S0-BFD-481

The Gingerbread Mansion Inn
presents

Cooking at the Inn with Chef Larry Martin

THE GINGERBREAD MANSION INN PRESENTS
COOKING AT THE INN WITH CHEF LARRY MARTIN

Book design by Silverstream, Inc.
Book cover design by Graphic Arts

ISBN: 0-9714144-0-8

Printed in the United States of America

10 9 8 7 6 5 4 3 2 1

Table of Contents

Warm Memories

Compiling the recipes for this cookbook has stirred up a wealth of warm memories for me. Remembering the happy times out at my Great Grandma's house searching for her Danish cookies in the kitchen cupboard under the stairs, watching Alma Jacobsen gently dipping chocolates at my grandparent's soda fountain and visiting with old friends enjoying their home baked goodies, are all memories that have come together to make this cookbook possible. Most of these family and friends are no longer with me, but thoughts of them live on as I prepare their recipes for guests visiting at the Inn.

Please come and enjoy these recipes with me and stir up some memories of your own.

Larry Martin
Chef, The Gingerbread Mansion Inn

Celebrating the Finest Accommodations

Johansens, an esteemed international publisher of guides to hotels, country houses, traditional inns, game lodges and business meeting venues, has selected Gingerbread Mansion Inn as the Most Excellent Inn in North America for the year 2001. This was the first major international acclaim the inn has received. To be awarded this certificate rewards a vision I have had to establish the Gingerbread Mansion Inn as world class lodging in the Victorian village of Ferndale.

Nothing at our inn exemplifies "world class" more than our chef Larry Martin. It is with great pleasure that I have the privilege of announcing the publishing of this cookbook, which represents the tip of the iceberg of Larry's talents. Larry's dedication to excellence is a major reason The Gingerbread Mansion Inn has attained it's highly regarded status. Now our guests and other food aficionados have access to Larry's favorite recipes.

So read on and enjoy!

Ken Torbert
Innkeeper, The Gingerbread Mansion Inn

Gourmet Breakfasts

Bright Beginnings: Beverages, Fruit, Granola

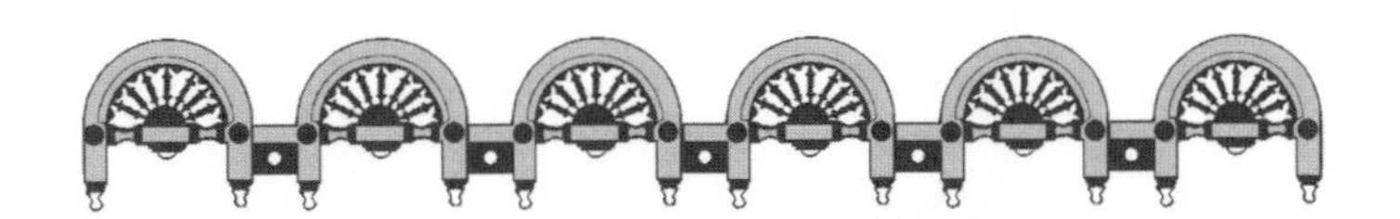

Peach Smoothie

6-8 large ripe peaches peeled and chopped
2 large oranges, juiced
½ cup honey
½ cup sour cream
fresh mint sprigs for garnish

In a blender, puree the peaches until smooth. Add orange juice and mix. Add honey and blend well. Add sour cream and blend until smooth.

Divide between 6 glasses and serve with a mint sprig.

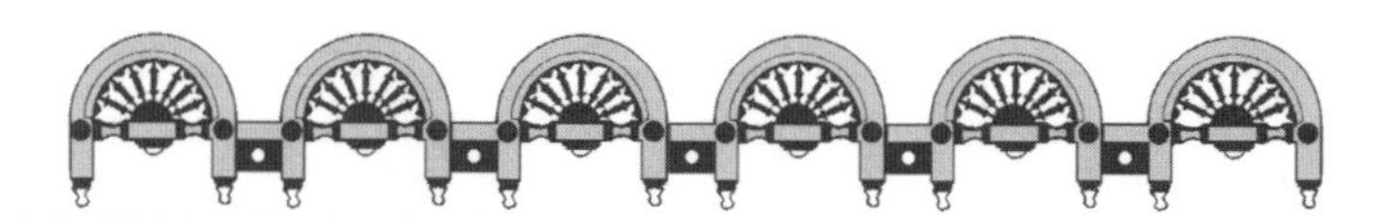

Cool Summertime Cappuccino

- 1 pint coffee-flavored ice cream
- 1 oz. B&B Liqueur (or more)
- 1 oz. crème de cocoa
- 2 T chocolate syrup
- ½ cup half and half
- ¼ t cinnamon

Mix all ingredients in blender until smooth. Pour into chilled stemmed glasses and garnish with whipped cream and shaved chocolate.

Serves 2.

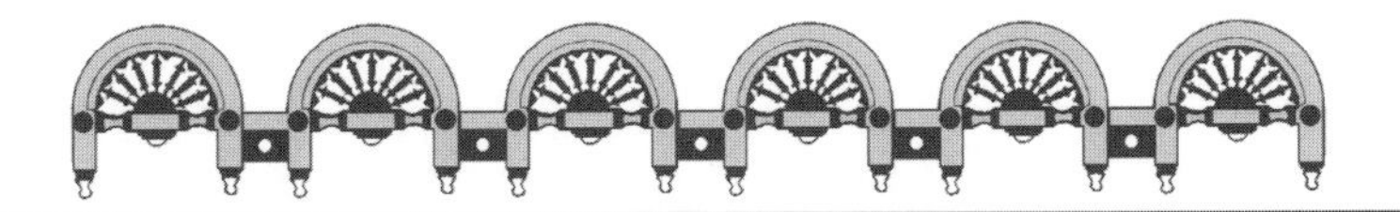

Rompope (Mexican Nog)

1 pint light rum
6 eggs
4 t sugar
1 pint orange juice
1 cup heavy cream
¼ t cinnamon

Combine all ingredients in large bowl of an electric mixer and beat until well blended. Chill thoroughly and serve in chilled glasses. Sprinkle lightly with more cinnamon if desired.

Makes 6-8 servings.

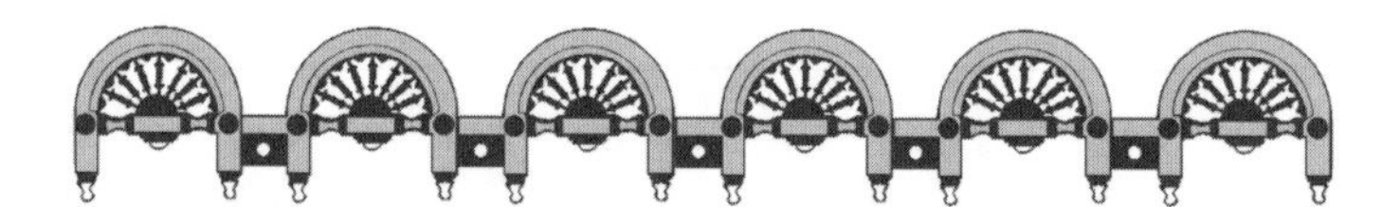

Hot Buttered Rum Batter

(A welcoming treat at holiday time)

Cream butter and sugars. Add the rest and mix well. Store in refrigerator. Will keep for up to 6 weeks.

For each cup of hot buttered rum, add one rounded tablespoons of batter and one jigger of light rum. Stir and garnish with nutmeg.

3 cubes unsalted butter
1 lb. light brown sugar
1 lb. super fine sugar
1 T vanilla
Grated peel of 1 lemon
¼ t cloves
½ t nutmeg
1 cup vanilla ice cream

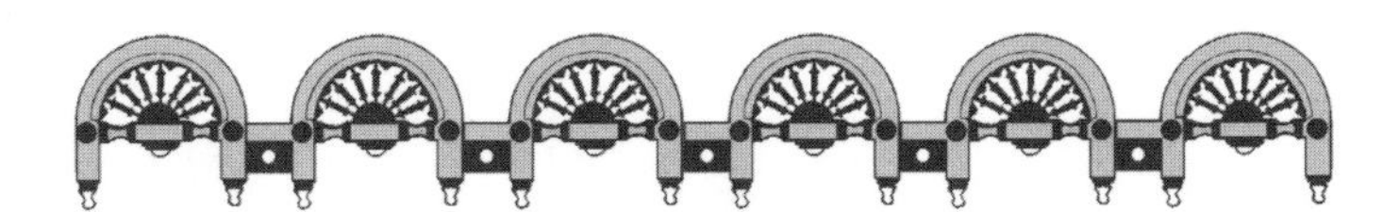

Apple Raisin Saute

2 t butter
2 large Golden Delicious apples, cored and cut into 1/3" slices
3/4 cup raisins
1/2 cup orange juice
1/3 cup apricot jam
1 t grated orange peel
1/2 t cinnamon
1/8 t allspice

Melt butter over medium heat in large non-stick skillet. Add apple slices. Cook, tossing occasionally, about 10 minutes, or until golden brown. Stir in remaining ingredients; cook about 3 minutes, stirring constantly, until sauce thickens slightly.

Pour over Stuffed French Toast or serve as a breakfast side dish.

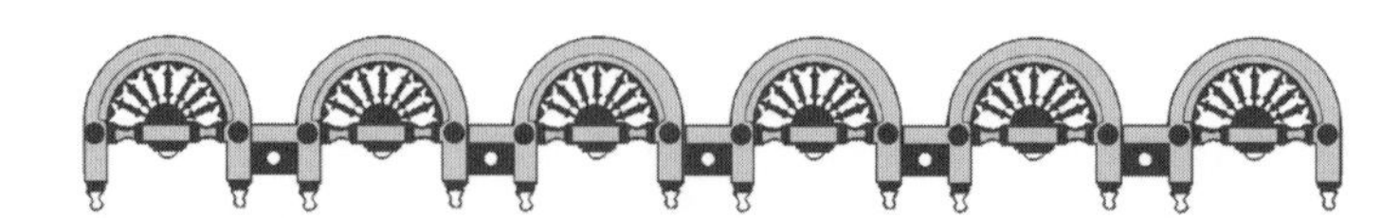

Baked Apples

Peel apples $2/3$ of the way down. Remove core and place in baking dish. In each apple place 2-4 pieces of candied fruit, 4-6 currants, 1 teaspoon butter, 1 teaspoon orange juice concentrate. Sprinkle some walnuts, cinnamon, cloves and sugar over top. Add small amount of water to bottom of dish.

Cover and bake 30-35 minutes. Spoon juice over apples. Serve hot or cold, with cream if desired.

Serves 4.

4 apples (Granny Smith, Rome or Pippin)
8-16 pieces candied fruit
16-24 currants
4 t butter
4 t frozen orange juice concentrate
4 t ground walnuts
4 t cinnamon
4 t cloves
4 t sugar
¼ t water

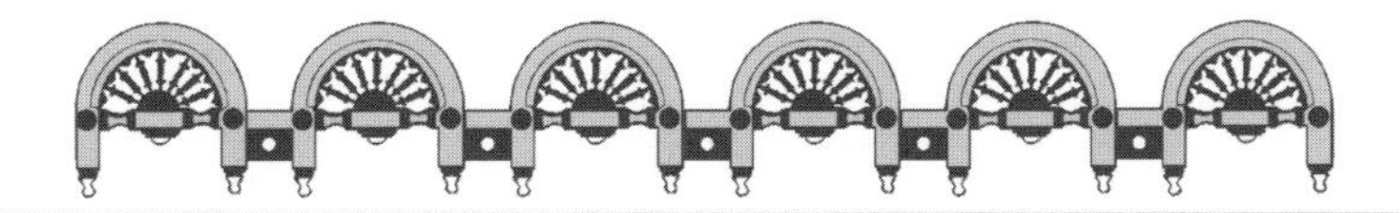

Chilled Fruit Soup

1 cup cranberry juice
½ cup orange juice
¼ t vanilla extract
1 cup apple juice
½ cup pineapple juice
½ cup strawberries
1 cup coarsely cut peaches
1 cup bananas
½ cup each: chopped bananas, seedless grapes, pineapple chunks, peaches and melon balls

In food processor, puree first 8 ingredients. Keep chilled. When ready to serve, add remaining fruit to the mixture. Serve in clear glass bowls. Garnish with a small dollop of sour cream and fresh mint leaves.

Yields 4 cups.

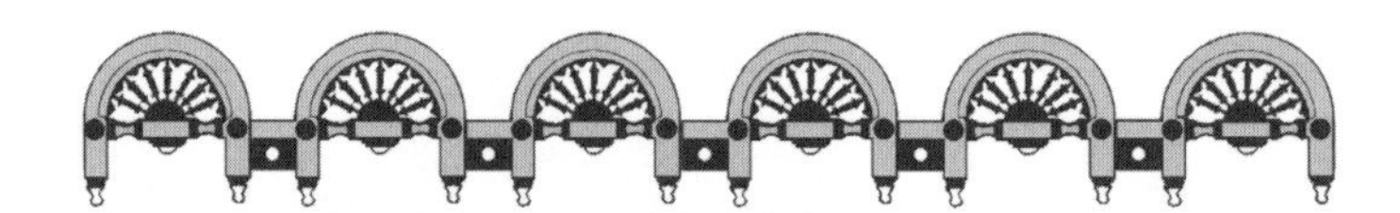

The Gingerbread Mansion's Special Granola

Warm honey, molasses and corn oil in saucepan. Add dry ingredients. Spread evenly on 2 cookie sheets; bake at 300° for 25-35 minutes.

Cool and store in refrigerator.

Makes 4½ pounds.

- 5-7 cups rolled oats
- 1 cup sunflower seeds
- 1 cup sesame seeds
- 1 cup (non-instant) dry milk
- 1 cup wheat germ
- 1 cup raisins or chopped dates
- 1 cup coconut
- 1 cup nuts
- 2 T cinnamon
- 1 cup honey
- 2 T molasses
- 1 cup corn oil

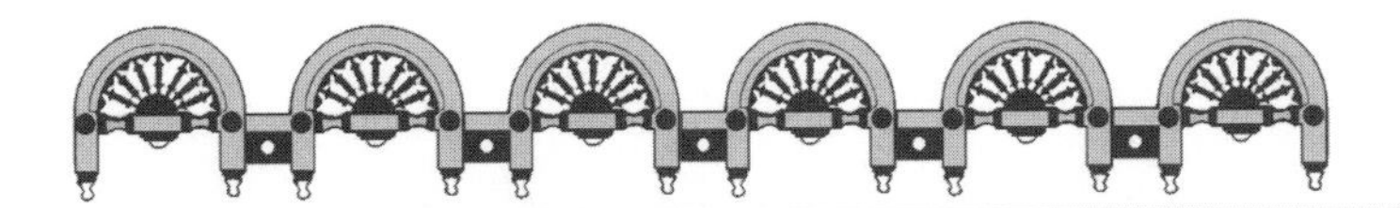

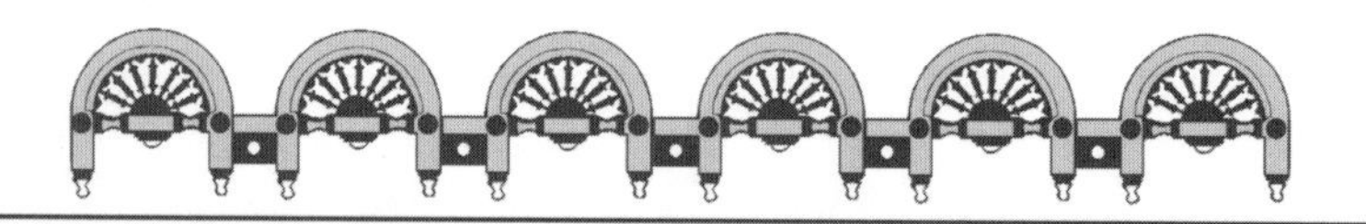

Rising to the Occasion: Breads, Coffee Cakes, Biscuits, Muffins

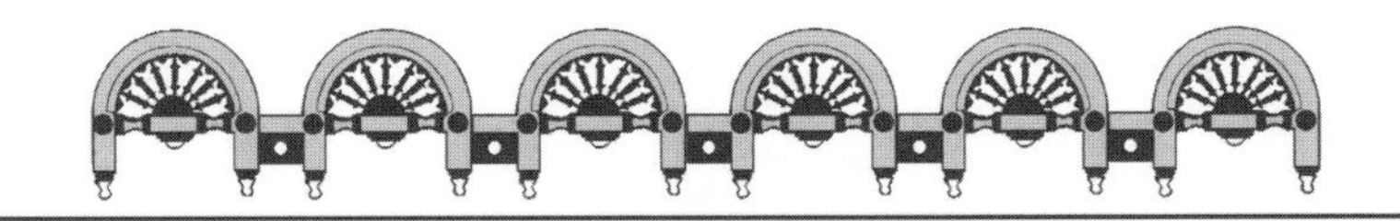

Orange Muffins

1 cup margarine
2 cups sugar
3 eggs
1½ t baking soda
1 t salt
1½ t cinnamon
2 T grated orange peel
1 t orange (or lemon) extract
½ cup orange juice
1 cup sour cream
3½ cups flour
¾ cup nuts

Combine wet ingredients and mix well. Add to combined dry ingredients.

Pour into greased muffin tins. Bake at 375° for 25 minutes.

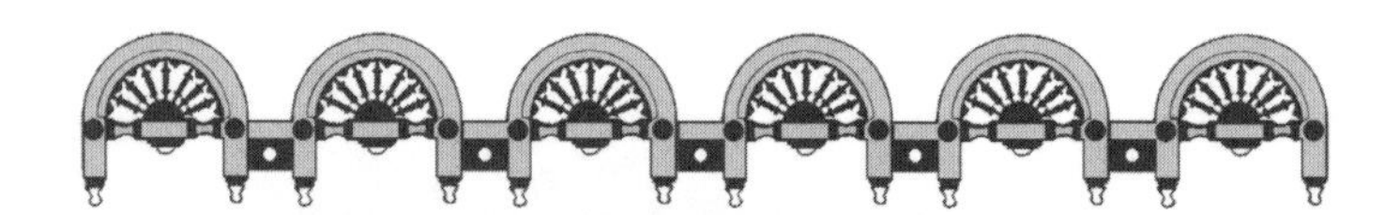

Pumpkin Buttermilk Muffins

Preheat oven to 350°. Mix together oil, sugar, eggs, pumpkin and buttermilk.

Add flour, baking powder, baking soda, cinnamon and allspice and beat until batter is smooth.

Stir in nuts and raisins. Spoon into greased muffin tins (3/4 full). Add Grapenuts to the top (optional) and bake for 30 minutes.

Makes 30 muffins.

- 1 cup vegetable oil
- 4 t baking powder
- 2 cups sugar
- 2 t baking soda
- 4 eggs
- 3 t ground cinnamon
- 2 cups canned pumpkin
- 1 t ground allspice
- 1 cup buttermilk
- 1½ cups chopped nuts
- 4 cups flour
- 2 cups raisins
- Grape Nuts for topping (optional)

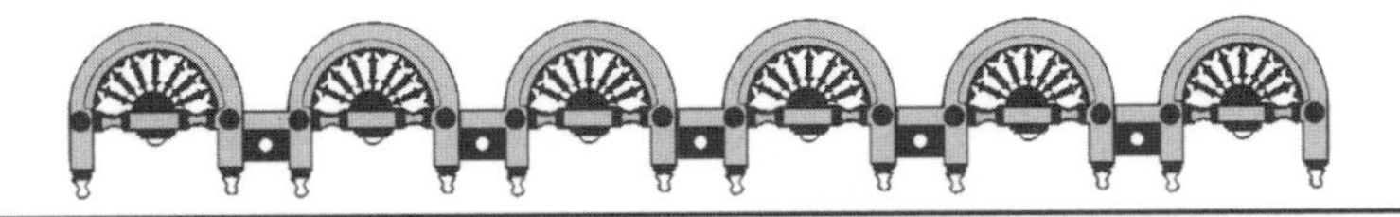

Blueberry Muffins

Very Good! Raspberry

Yields 12
2 cups flour
¾ cup sugar
1½ t baking powder
½ t baking soda
1 cup blueberries*
½ t salt
1 cup buttermilk
⅓ cup oil
1 egg

Yields 24
4 cups flour
1 ½ cups sugar
3 t baking powder
1 t baking soda
2 cups blueberries*
1 t salt
2 cups buttermilk
⅔ cup oil
2 eggs

*may substitute fresh or unthawed raspberries for blueberries

Combine wet ingredients, mixing well. Add to dry ingredients, mixing until just blended. Pour into greased muffin tins, and bake at 375° for 20-25 minutes.

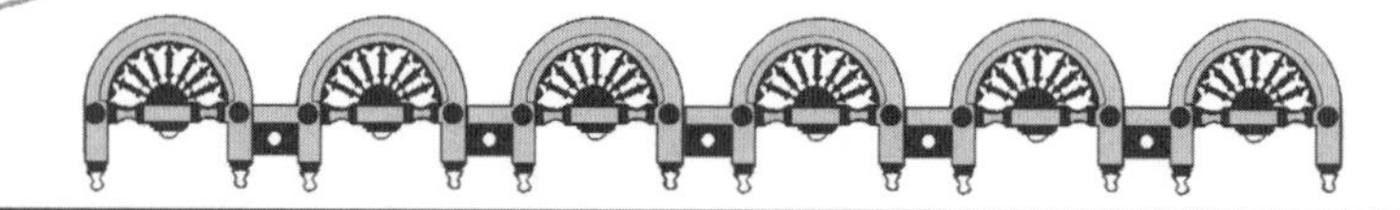

Orange Pecan Muffins

1 grated peel of orange
1 cube butter, softened
¾ cup pecans, coarsely chopped
1 cup sugar
2 eggs
1 t baking soda
2 cups flour
1 cup plain yogurt
½ cup orange juice

Grease muffin tin. Set aside. Grate orange peel and chop pecans.

Beat butter into sugar until pale and creamy. Beat in eggs. Stir in baking soda and orange peel. Alternately fold in flour and yogurt. Fold in pecans.

Bake 20 minutes at 375° or until browned. Remove from pan while still warm and brush with orange juice and sprinkle with sugar.

Yields 1 dozen.

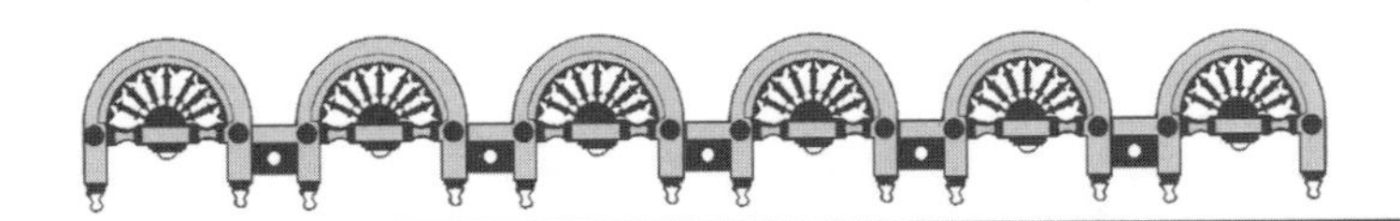

Bran Muffins

1 cup Kelloggs Bran Buds
2 cups Kelloggs All Bran
1 cup water
½ cup butter
1½ cups sugar
2 beaten eggs
2 cups buttermilk
2 cups whole wheat flour
1 t baking soda

Put Kelloggs Bran Buds in boiling water. Set aside to cool.

Cream butter with sugar. Add eggs and buttermilk. Sift together flour and baking soda and add to mix. Add Kelloggs All Bran and cooled bran buds. Mix well.

Fill greased muffin tins 2/3 full. Bake at 400° for 15 minutes.

Makes 5 dozen.

Batter will keep for 2-3 weeks in the refrigerator. You can also add raisins to this recipe if desired.

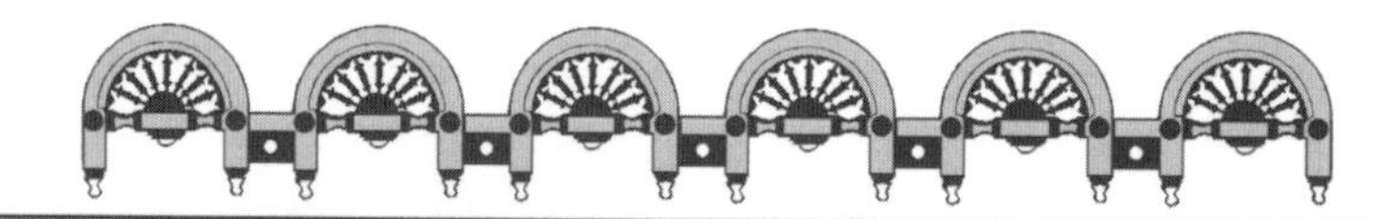

Carrot-Wheat Muffins

1 cup flour
1 cup whole wheat flour
$2\frac{1}{2}$ t baking powder
$\frac{1}{2}$ t baking soda
1 t cinnamon
$\frac{1}{4}$ cup milk
$\frac{1}{4}$ cup honey
$\frac{1}{4}$ cup oil
1 egg
1 cup shredded carrots
$\frac{1}{2}$ cup raisins

Mix dry ingredients and carrots and raisins. Set aside.

Combine remaining ingredients. Stir milk mixture into flour mixture just until all ingredients are moistened. Spoon into greased tins.

Bake 20 minutes at 375°.

Yields 1 dozen muffins.

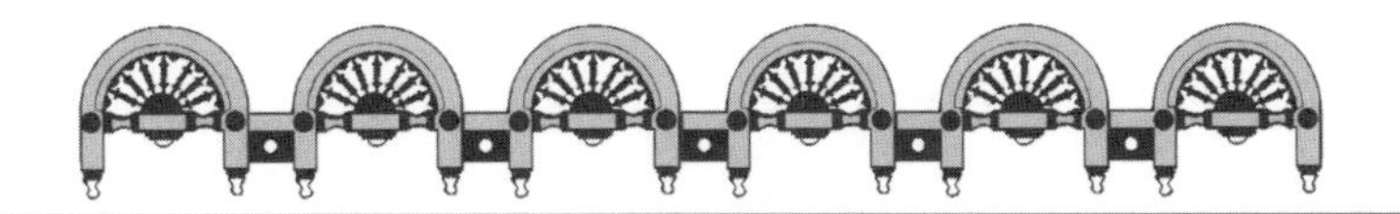

Cheddar Cheese Muffins

- 2 cups flour
- 3 T sugar
- 3 t baking powder
- ½ t salt
- 3 T butter, softened
- 1 cup milk
- 1 egg
- 1½ cups cheddar cheese, grated
- ½ cup powdered sugar for dusting

Grease and flour 12 muffin tins. Preheat oven to 400°. Mix flour, baking powder, sugar and salt in bowl. Put egg, milk and butter in food processor; cover and process until mixture is smooth, stir in cheese.

Pour wet ingredients into dry and combine until mixture is just moistened. Bake in tins 20-25 minutes. Dust with powdered sugar before serving. Makes 12 muffins.

Note: For Herbed Cheese Muffins, add a pinch or oregano, basil, parsley, pepper and paprika.

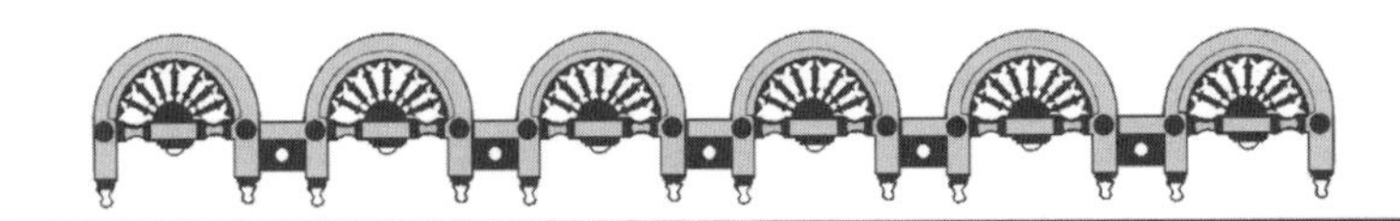

Sour Cream Biscuits

Mix flour and baking powder; cut in butter with pastry blender until mixture resembles coarse meal. Add sour cream and milk and mix until just blended. Turn out on floured surface and knead gently several times.

Roll out to ½ to ¾ inch thickness and cut out biscuits with 2½ inch cutter. Place on lightly greased sheet. Brush tops with additional melted butter before baking. Bake in 400° oven for 8-10 minutes.

Yield 12-15
2 ½ cups flour
1 T baking powder
½ cup butter
⅔ cup sour cream
½ cup milk

Yield 18-20
3 ¾ cups flour
4 ½ t baking powder
¾ cup butter
1 cup sour cream
¾ cup milk

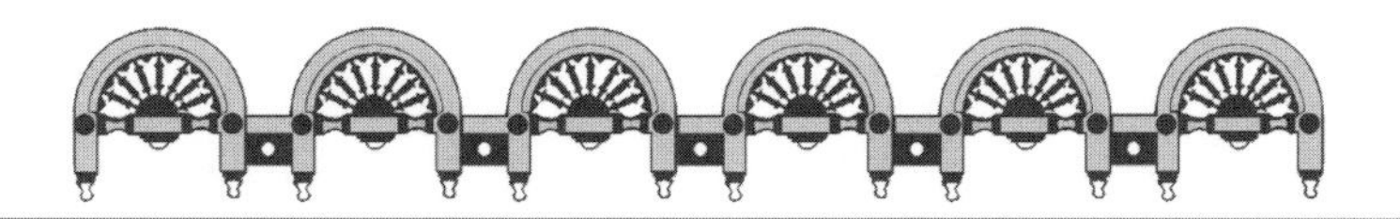

Cheddar Cheese Biscuits

Yield 12
2 cups flour
1 T sugar
2 ½ t baking powder
1 t pepper
½ t baking soda
½ t salt
6 T chilled, unsalted butter, cut into small pieces
1¼ cups grated cheddar cheese
1 cup buttermilk
poppy seeds

Yield 18
3 cups flour
1½ T sugar
3¾ t baking powder
1½ t pepper
¾ t baking soda
¾ t salt
9 T chilled, unsalted butter, cut into small pieces
2 cups grated cheddar cheese
1½ cups buttermilk
poppy seeds

Combine first 6 ingredients and blend. Add butter and cut in. Mix in cheese. Mix enough buttermilk into flour mixture to bind dough. Turn out on floured surface and knead about 10 turns. Pat dough out to ¾" thick; cut with a 2½" cutter and put on ungreased sheet. Brush with glaze and sprinkle with poppy seeds. Bake at 400° for 10 minutes.

Glaze
Beat 1 egg with 1 tablespoon of milk.

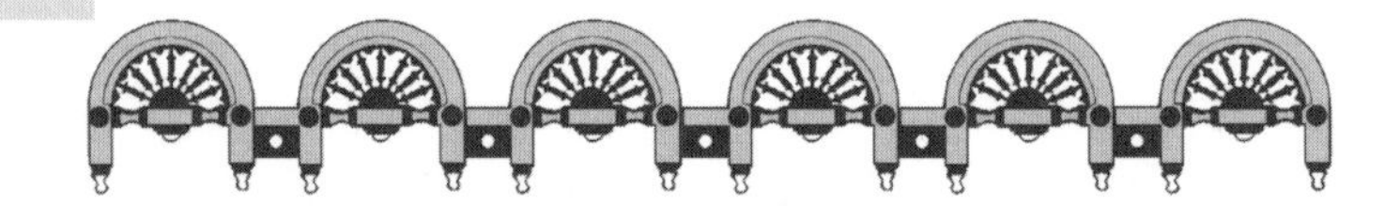

Cake Doughnuts

Cream butter and sugar. Add eggs, then milk, vanilla and flour, in which baking powder, salt and nutmeg have been added. Roll out on floured board to ½" thickness and cut with doughnut cutter 2½" size.

Fry doughnuts and holes in a frying pan half filled with cooking oil that has reached a temperature of 375°. Turn them over as they rise to the surface and brown to a medium golden color. Drain on paper towels. Sprinkle with granulated sugar if desired.

- 3 eggs, slightly beaten
- 1 cup sugar
- 4 T butter, softened
- 1 cup milk
- 1 t vanilla
- 4 cups flour
- 4 t baking powder
- ¼ t salt
- 1 t nutmeg

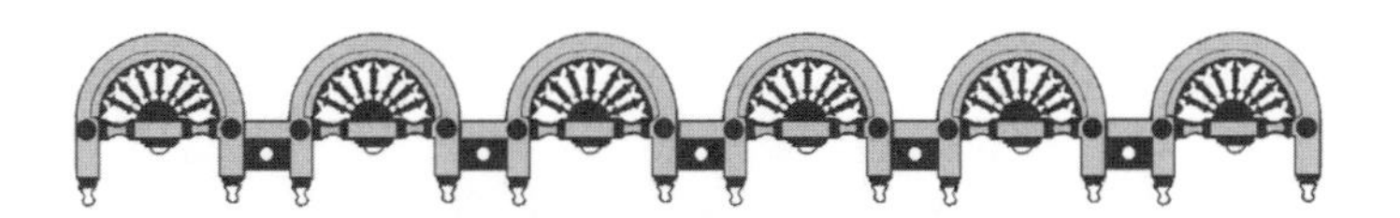

Erla's Prune Ladder

- ¾ cup butter
- 2 cups milk
- 1¼ cups sugar
- 2 pkgs. dry yeast dissolved in a little warm water with 1 teaspoon of sugar
- 3 eggs yolks, beaten
- 1½ t vanilla
- 5 cups flour
- 1¼ t salt
- 2½-3 cups pitted prunes
- ½ t cinnamon

Cook prunes until soft in a little water. Chop and add ½ cup sugar and cinnamon. Set aside.

Heat butter and milk until scalding. Put into large mixing bowl. Add remaining sugar and stir to dissolve. Cool to lukewarm. Add dissolved yeast and mix to combine. Add eggs, vanilla, flour and salt. Add enough flour to make a soft dough. Beat dough for about 10 minutes, adding a little extra flour if needed. Transfer to greased bowl and let rise until doubled in bulk, 1 to 2 hours.

Divide dough in half. Roll each half on lightly floured board into a rectangle that is ½ inch thick. Brush each with prune mixture and fold edges and end toward center and turn over onto greased sheet. Cut slits across the top. Let rise until doubled, about 1 hour.

Bake at 350° for about 20-25 minutes. Cool slightly then drizzle with a mixture of confectioners sugar and a little milk.

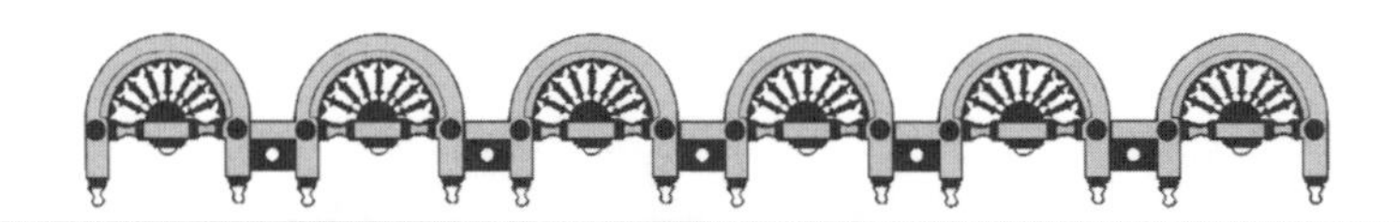

Mincemeat Braid

1 cup mincemeat
½ cup chopped, peeled apple (Granny Smith or Golden Delicious)
⅓ cup chopped walnuts
3 to 4 cups flour
1 pkg. active dry yeast
1 cup milk
¼ cup sugar
¼ cup butter
½ t salt
1 egg
1 T lemon zest

In a small mixing bowl, stir together mincemeat, apples and nuts. Set aside.

In a large mixer bowl combine 1½ cups of the flour and the yeast. In a small saucepan, heat milk, sugar, butter and salt until warm, 120° and butter is almost melted. Stir constantly. Add to flour mixture. Add egg and lemon zest. Beat on low speed for 30 seconds, scraping bowl. Then beat on high for 3 minutes. Gradually add enough remaining flour to make a soft dough, then turn out on floured surface and knead in remaining flour. Knead for 3-5 minutes, until smooth and elastic. Place in greased bowl and turn to coat.

Cover and let rise in a warm place until doubled. About 45 minutes. Punch dough down. Divide in half. Cover and let rise 10 minutes. Divide each half into 3 portions. Roll 1 portion into a 12x4" rectangle. Spread with 3 tablespoons of mincemeat mixture. Roll up and seal edges. Place on greased baking sheet. Repeat with 2 more portions of dough and mincemeat. Braid the 3 strips together and seal ends. Repeat with remaining dough and mincemeat to make second braid.

Cover and let rise until nearly double in bulk, 45 minutes. Bake at 350° for 25-30 minutes.

Makes 2 loaves.

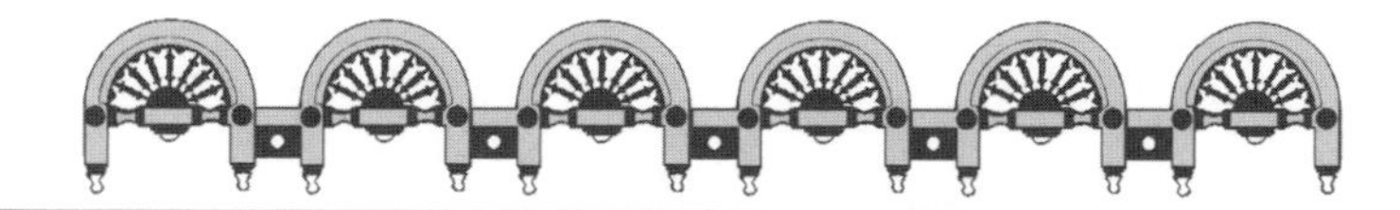

Cinnamon Buns

2 pkgs. dry yeast
1 T sugar
1 cup lukewarm water
1 cup milk, scalded and cooled
6 ½ cups flour
1 T butter, softened
½ cup sugar
3 eggs, well beaten
1 t salt

Glaze
2 T butter
1 T milk
1 t vanilla
2 cups sifted confectioners sugar

Dissolve yeast and 1 tablespoon sugar in lukewarm water. Add milk and 3 cups flour. Beat until smooth. Cream butter and sugar in another bowl. Add to yeast mixture. Add eggs, salt and remaining flour to make a soft dough. Turn out onto floured board and knead lightly. Place in greased bowl. Cover and let rise in a warm place until doubled in bulk, at least one hour or more.

Turn out on floured board and knead down. Roll out into a rectangle to about ¼ inch thickness. Brush with some additional butter, that has been melted. Sprinkle with a mixture of brown sugar, cinnamon and raisins or currants. Roll up lengthwise. Cut into sections about 1" in width and place on a greased baking sheet. Cut edges down. Cover and let rise about 1 hour or until doubled.

Before baking, brush with melted butter. Bake in 375° oven about 20 minutes. When done, remove from oven and let cool about 10 minutes, then glaze with the following mixture.

Glaze

Beat all ingredients in electric mixer until light and fluffy.

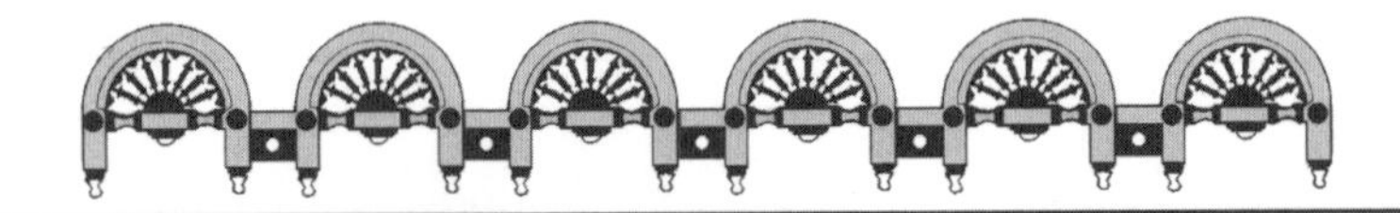

Orange-Glazed Chocolate Orange Sweet Rolls

Butter two 9" diameter cake pans. Set aside. Combine milk, ¼ cup orange juice and 4 tablespoons butter in heavy saucepan. Stir over medium heat until registers 120°F on thermometer. Whisk eggs, ¼ cup sugar, orange peel and salt in large bowl. Gradually whisk in heated milk mixture. Add yeast, then flour, mixing until dough is moist. Knead dough on floured surface until smooth and elastic, about 5 minutes. Place dough in lightly oiled bowl and turn to coat. Cover and let rise in warm place until doubled in bulk, about 1 hour.

Punch dough down and divide in half. Roll one piece on a floured surface into a 12x18" rectangle. Spread with 3 tablespoons butter. Sprinkle evenly with 1/3 cup chocolate chips and ¼ cup sugar. Roll up from long side. Pinch at seam to seal. Slice into 12 rolls and place rolls, cut side down, in single layer in prepared pan. Repeat process with remaining dough. Cover rolls loosely and let rise until doubled, 45 minutes to 1 hour.

Preheat oven to 375°. Stir cream and Grand Marnier together. Drizzle evenly over rolls. Bake until rolls are puffed and golden, about 25 minutes. Cool 15 minutes. Whisk confectioners sugar with enough orange juice to make a thick glaze, adding 1 tablespoon juice at a time. Remove rolls from pan and spread with glaze.

- ¾ cup whole milk
- ¼ cup plus 3 T orange juice
- 10 T unsalted butter, softened
- 2 large eggs
- ¾ cup sugar
- 1 T grated orange peel
- 1 t salt
- 1 T yeast
- 4 cups flour
- 2/3 cup semi-sweet chocolate chips
- ½ cup whipping cream
- 2 T Grand Marnier or orange juice
- 1 ¼ cups confectioners sugar

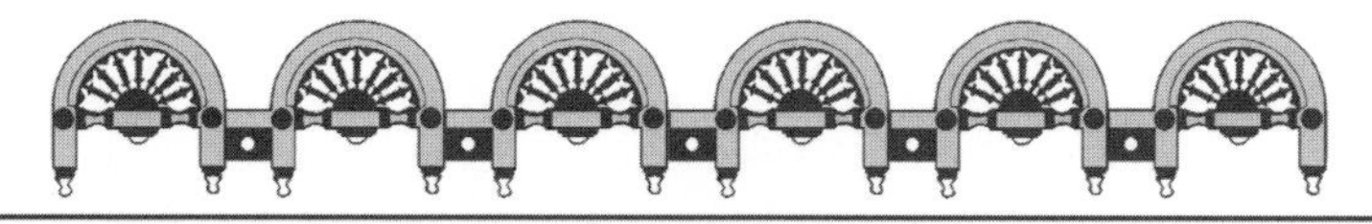

Jerry's Italian Easter Bread

- 2¾ to 3¾ cups unsifted flour
- ¼ cup sugar
- 1 t salt
- 1 pkg. active dry yeast
- ⅔ cup milk
- 2 T butter
- 2 eggs, room temperature
- ½ cup mixed candied fruit
- ¼ cup chopped blanched almonds
- ½ t anise seed
- 3 T melted butter
- 5 colored raw eggs
- Confectioners sugar icing
- Colored sprinkles

In a large bowl, combine 1 cup flour, sugar, salt and undissolved yeast. Heat milk and 2 tablespoons butter in a saucepan over low heat until liquid is warm (120°-130°F). Add to dry ingredients; beat for 2 minutes at medium speed, scrapping bowl occasionally. Add 2 eggs and ½ cup flour. Beat at high speed 2 minutes. Stir in enough additional flour to make a soft dough. Turn out on a floured board and knead for 10 minutes. Place in greased bowl and turn to coat. Cover and let rise for one hour or until double in bulk.

Punch dough down, turn onto floured board. Knead in fruits, almonds and anise seed. Divide in half. Roll each piece of dough into a 24 inch rope. Twist ropes together loosely. Form into a ring on a greased baking sheet. Brush with melted butter. Place colored eggs into spaces in the twist. Cover and let rise until doubled, about 1 hour.

Bake at 350° for 30-35 minutes or until done. Remove from baking sheet and cool. Frost ring with a mixture of confectioners sugar and milk and sprinkle with colored sprinkles.

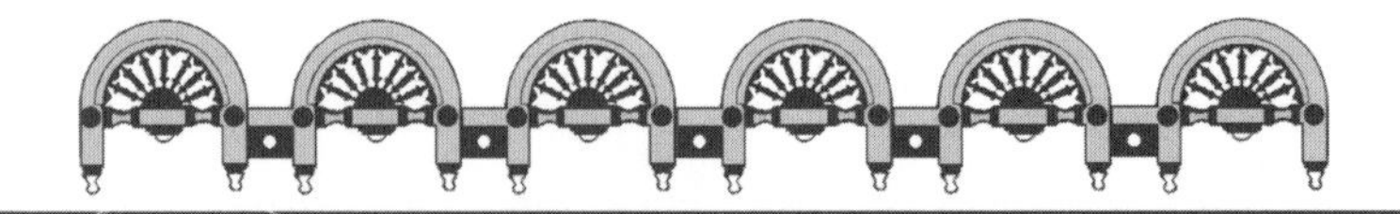

Ida's Portuguese Sweet Rolls

Measure flour into a large bowl. Mix sugar and salt into small bowl and set aside. Sprinkle the 3 packages of yeast into ¾ cup of warm water and add the 2 tablespoons sugar and 1 cup of flour. Mix to make a soft sponge. Set aside to let rise for 10-15 minutes.

Break eggs into a medium bowl and beat well. Set aside. Add 1 ¾ cups milk and ¼ cup water to a saucepan and heat to boiling. Slowly pour the sugar and salt mixture into the liquid, stirring while pouring. Lower heat and cook for about 5 minutes. Slowly pour the milk mixture into the beaten eggs. Stirring as you pour so the eggs won't cook.

Make a well in the center of the flour bowl. Pour 1/3 of the egg mixture into the flour well and stir until absorbed. Repeat twice and on the last addition, pour in the yeast mixture and mix well with hands; kneading until the dough is well mixed and elastic. In three additions, add the melted butter, mixing well after each addition. Once incorporated, knead well in the bowl, pulling the dough away from sides of the bowl and folding over the top. Sprinkle top lightly with flour, cover and let rise until doubled in bulk (about 1 hour). Punch down and let rise again. After second rising, shape dough into rolls 2-2½ inches in diameter and place on lightly greased baking sheets. Let rise in a warm place, covered, for about 30 minutes or until well risen. Test by pressing your finger into a roll. If it leaves an indentation, it's ready. Bake at 350° for 12-15 minutes or until golden.

Makes about 4 dozen rolls.

12 cups flour
2½ cups sugar
2 t salt
8 brown eggs
1 cup butter, melted
1 ¾ cup milk
¼ cup water
3 pkgs. yeast
¾ cup warm water
2 T sugar
1 cup flour

Hedevige (Danish Coffee Buns)

1 cup boiling water
1 cup butter
¾ cup sugar
1 pkg dry yeast
1 t vanilla
3 eggs, slightly beaten
¾ cup raisins
4½ cups flour
1 pinch of salt
½ t cinnamon
½ t nutmeg

Pour boiling water on butter. When butter is melted add yeast. Mix to dissolve yeast, then add sugar, beaten eggs, flavoring, flour and cinnamon, nutmeg and raisins. Stir until well blended. Turn out into well-greased bowl and cover. Let rise until doubled in bulk, about 1 hour. Stir down and drop by tablespoonsful onto a greased cookie sheet. Let rise about 1 hour. Cover with additional melted butter and sprinkle with sugar.

Bake in 375° oven for 15 minutes or until lightly browned.

Yields about 3 dozen buns.

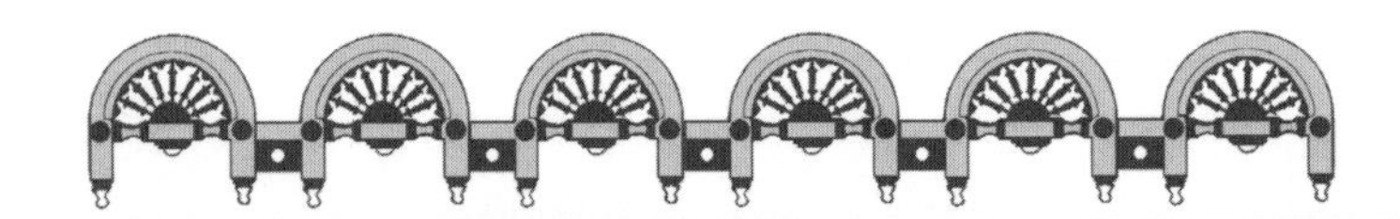

Breakfast Puffs

In mixing bowl, combine flour, baking powder, salt and mace. In bowl of electric mixer, beat together ½ cup sugar, oil, egg and vanilla on medium speed for 30 seconds. Add flour mixture and milk alternately to egg mixture, beating on low speed after each addition, just until combined. Fill 1 dozen muffin tins 2/3 full of batter.

Bake in 350° oven for 15-20 minutes or until firm and golden. Meanwhile in bowl, combine remaining ½ cup sugar and cinnamon. Remove muffins from tin and while still hot roll in melted butter, then in cinnamon-sugar mixture. Serve with butter and jelly.

1½ cups flour
1½ t baking powder
½ t salt
¼ t mace
1 cup sugar, divided
1/3 cup vegetable oil
1 egg
1 t vanilla
½ cup milk
1 t cinnamon
6 T butter, melted

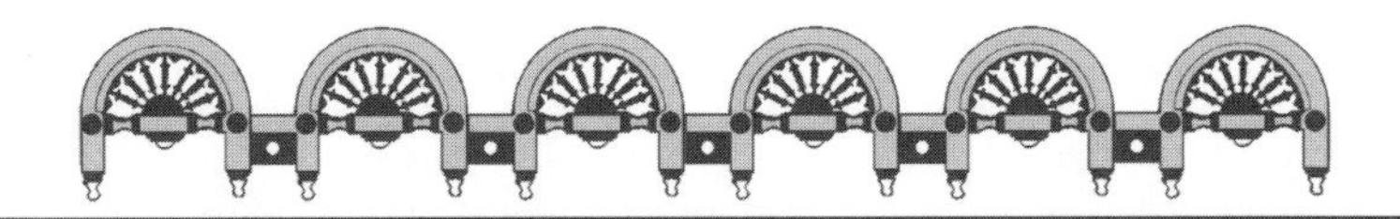

Magda's Swedish Cream Dough

- 1 package of yeast
- ¼ cup warm water
- 3⅓ cups flour
- ¼ cup sugar
- 1 t salt
- ½ cup chilled butter
- 1 cup cream
- ½ cup evaporated milk
- 3 eggs (separated)
- handful of raisins or candied fruit

Dissolve yeast in warm water. Let stand for 5 minutes.

Stir together flour, sugar and salt. Cut in chilled butter.

Mix yeast with cream, evaporated milk, and egg yolks. Stir yeast mixture into flour mixture. Grease a clean bowl and turn dough to coat. Cover with plastic wrap and refrigerate overnight. Knead lightly on floured board. Can either make buns or cinnamon rolls. See cinnamon rolls.

For buns, add a handful of raisins or candied fruit and mix into dough. Shape dough into 18 2" round balls. Brush with egg whites and place on a greased tray, cover and let rise in a warm spot until doubled in size. About 1 hour.

Bake in 350° oven for 25-30 minutes or until golden.

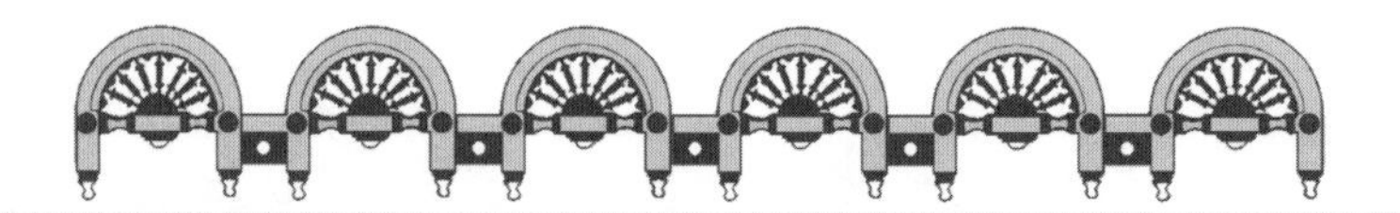

Lemon Blueberry Bundt Cake

Mix all ingredients well. Fold in 2 cups blueberries. Bake at 350° for 1 hour.

- 4 cups yellow cake mix
- 3 eggs
- ¾ cup water
- ½ cup oil
- 1 cup sour cream
- ¼ cup vanilla pudding mix
- 1 t lemon extract

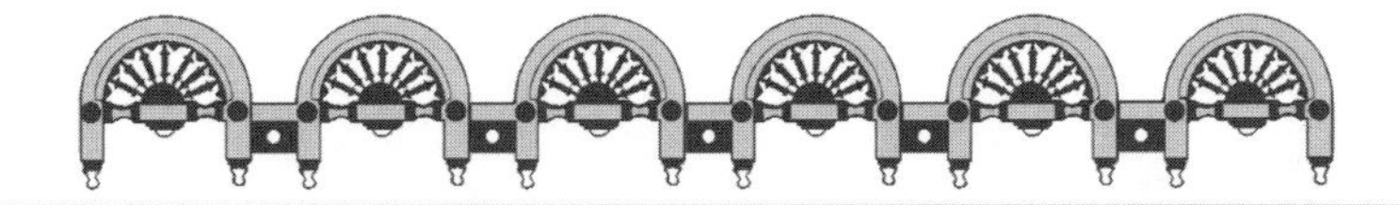

Sunrise Serenade Coffee Cake

- 2½-3 cups unbleached or bread flour
- 1 package active dry yeast
- 1 t baking powder
- ⅓ cup sour cream
- ⅓ cup orange juice
- ¼ cup sugar
- ¼ cup butter
- 1 t salt
- 1 egg
- 1 t grated orange peel
- raspberry currant or strawberry jelly
- orange glaze (recipe follows)
- ¼ cup sliced almonds, toasted

Orange Glaze

- 1¼ cups confectioner's sugar, sifted
- ⅛ t almond extract
- 1 t grated orange peel
- 1 T orange juice

In large mixer bowl combine 1 cup flour, yeast and baking powder. In saucepan, heat sour cream, orange juice, sugar, butter and salt until very warm (120°-130°), and butter is almost melted, stirring constantly. Stir heated mixture into flour mixture. Add egg and orange peel. Beat with electric mixer on low speed for 1 minute, scrapping sides of bowl. Beat for 3 minutes on high speed. Stir in as much remaining flour as you can by hand with a spoon. Turn dough out onto a lightly floured surface, knead in enough remaining flour to make a smooth elastic and moderately soft dough. Shape into ball. Cover with dish towel and let rest for 15 minutes.

To shape, roll out dough to form a 10x10" square. With floured cutter, cut into 12 doughnuts, using doughnut cutter. On greased baking sheet arrange doughnut shapes in circle. Stretch the doughnuts lightly with fingers to elongate them slightly. Cluster the holes from the rings in the center, cutting additional holes from the scraps. Let dough rise until double, about 1 hour.

Bake at 375° for 10-12 minutes or until golden. Carefully remove coffee cake from baking sheet to wire rack. Brush with melted butter and allow to cool. Spoon desired jelly into centers of doughnut rings. Drizzle orange glaze over cake and sprinkle centers with toasted almonds.

Orange Glaze

In mixing bowl, stir together combine all ingredients.

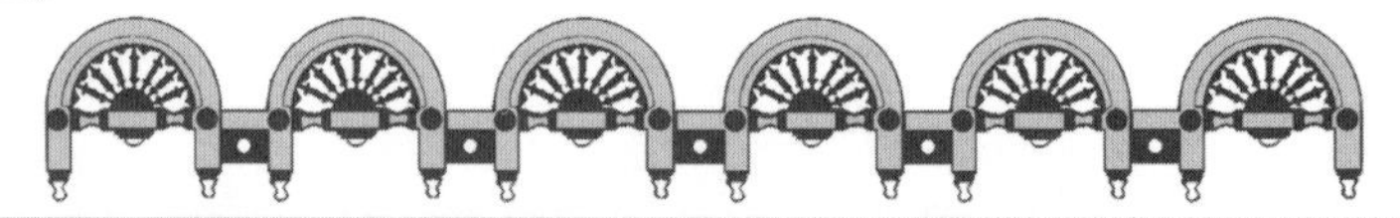

Overnight Coffee Cake

2 cups sifted flour
1 t baking powder
1 t baking soda
1 t cinnamon
½ t salt
⅔ cup butter or margarine
1 cup sugar
½ cup brown sugar, firmly packed
2 eggs
1 cup buttermilk
½ cup brown sugar firmly packed
½ cup chopped walnut or pecans
½ t ground cinnamon
¼ t ground nutmeg

Sift together flour, baking powder, baking soda, 1 teaspoon cinnamon and salt.

Cream together butter, sugar and ½ cup brown sugar until light and fluffy. Add eggs, one at a time, beating well after each addition. Add dry ingredients alternately with buttermilk, beating well after each addition. Spread batter in a greased and floured 13x9x2" baking pan. Combine ½ cup brown sugar, nuts, ½ teaspoon cinnamon and nutmeg; mix well. Sprinkle over batter. Refrigerate 8 hours or overnight.

Bake in a 350° oven 45 minutes or until done. Cut in squares and serve warm.

Serves 16.

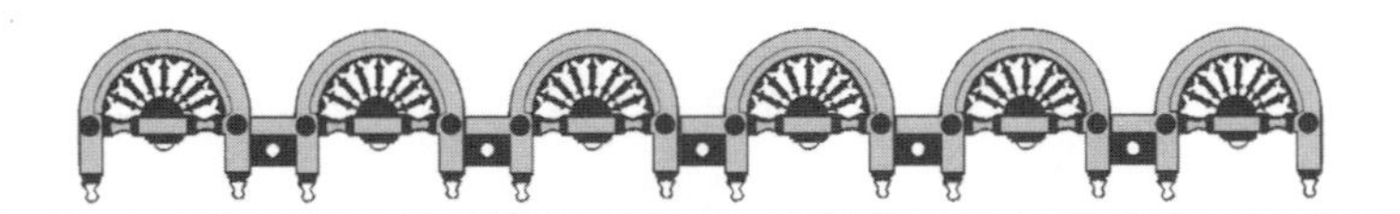

Sour Cream Poppy Seed Cake

4 cups lemon cake mix
3 eggs
½ cup dry sherry
½ cup oil
1 cup sour cream
¼ cup poppy seeds
1 scoop vanilla pudding mix
½ cup water

Mix well and bake at 350° for 50 minutes. Watch carefully after 45 minutes. Doesn't have to cook more than 50 minutes.

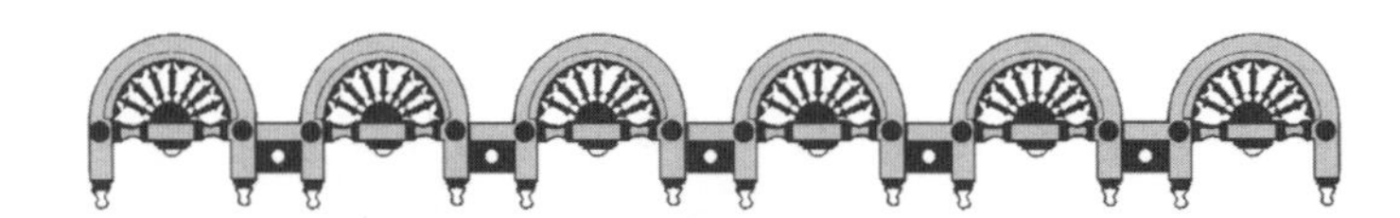

Sour Cream Coffee Cake

Mix all cake ingredients until well blended (batter will be thick). Mix all filling ingredients until well blended. Layer 1/3 batter, ½ filling, 1/3 batter, ½ filling, 1/3 batter.

Bake at 350° for approximately 1 hour.

Cake
1 cup butter
1½ cups sugar
3 eggs
1 t vanilla extract
1 t almond extract
1½ t baking soda
1½ t baking powder
1 t salt
3 cups flour
2 cups (1 large container) sour cream

Filling
½ cup brown sugar
½ cup finely chopped nuts
1½ t cinnamon

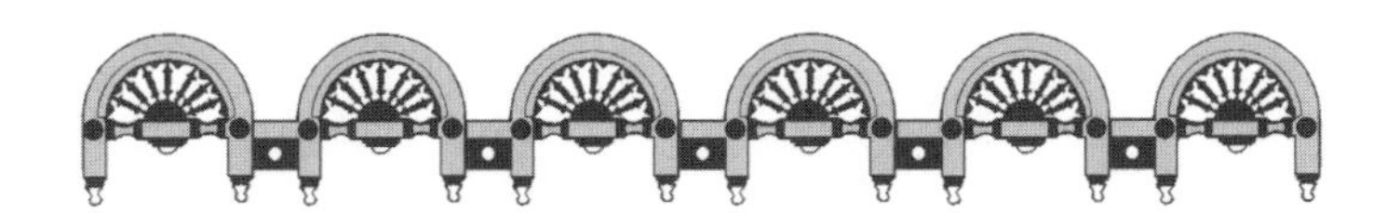

Spiced Banana Bundt Cake

3 cups flour
1 t soda
1 t cinnamon
2 cups sugar
1 t salt
1 ½ cups oil
1 8 oz. can crushed pineapple (don't drain)
1 ½ t vanilla
3 eggs
2 cups diced bananas
1 cup chopped pecans

Sift dry ingredients and add the rest, mixing by hand until just blended. Pour into greased tube (Bundt) pan and bake for 1 hour at 350°.

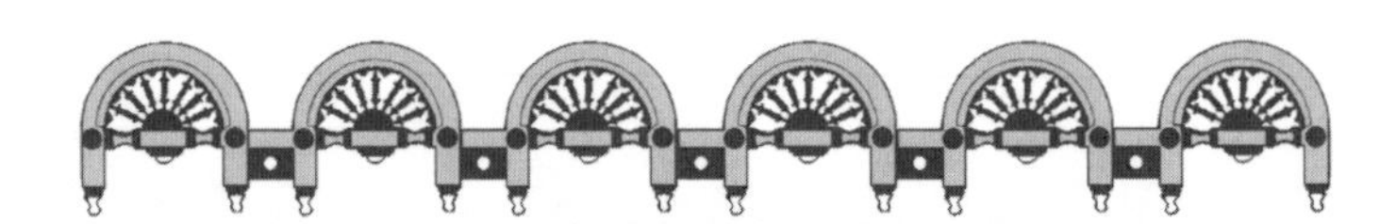

Sunshine Breakfast Bread

Combine prunes, nuts, brown sugar and cinnamon; set aside. In mixing bowl, cream sugar and butter until light and fluffy. Add eggs one at a time, beating well after each addition. Combine yogurt, orange peel and vanilla; set aside. Sift together flour; baking powder, baking soda and salt in medium bowl. Add to creamed mixture alternately with yogurt mixture.

Spread one half of batter evenly into greased and floured bundt cake ban. Sprinkle with half the prune-nut mixture. Repeat with remaining batter and prune-nut mixture. Gently run a knife through the batter to mix the batter and prune-nut mixture, being careful to only run the knife around once.

Bake at 350° for 50-60 minutes.

Cool in pan 5 minutes. Loosen and invert onto rack.

- 1 cup (about 6 oz.) pitted prunes, coarsely chopped
- ½ cup chopped nuts
- 2 T firmly packed brown sugar
- 1 t cinnamon
- 1 ½ t sugar
- ¾ cup butter, softened
- 2 eggs
- 1 cup unflavored yogurt
- 2 T grated orange peel
- 1 t vanilla
- 2¼ cups flour
- 2 t baking powder
- ½ t baking soda
- ½ t salt

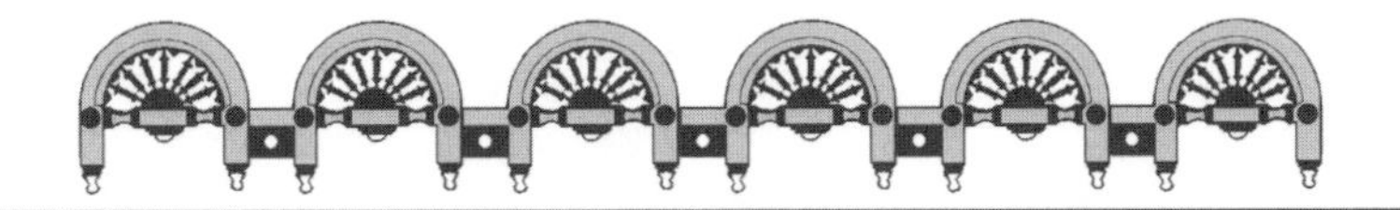

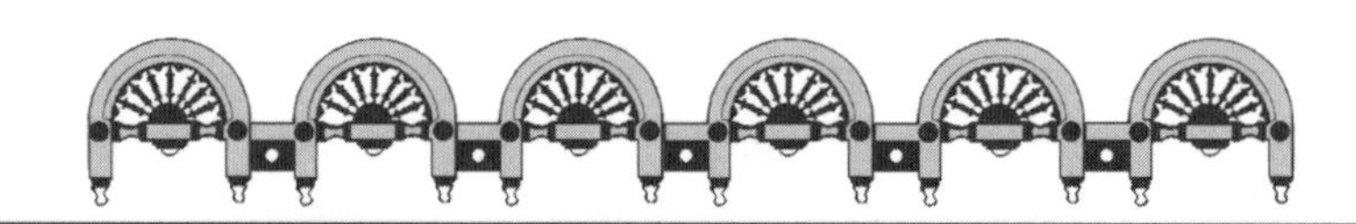

Exciting Entrees: From Sweet to Savory

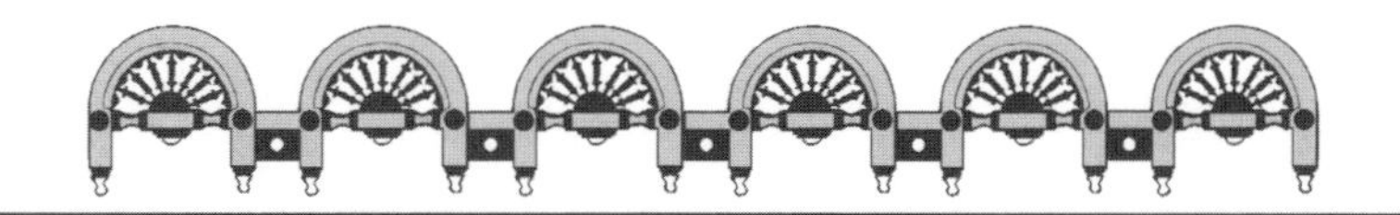

Panetone French Toast With Cinnamon-Raisin Sauce

6 eggs
1 ½ cups half & half
¾ cup heavy cream
¼ cup dark rum
8 T sugar
3 t vanilla
¼ t cinnamon
¼ t nutmeg
2 cups corn flakes, crushed
8 slices day-old panetone
(Italian-style fruit bread)
1½ t orange peel
butter

Cinnamon-Raisin Sauce
2 T butter
1 T flour
1 cup water
1 cup sugar
1 t vanilla
1 t cinnamon
½ cup raisins

Beat eggs slightly, add creams, sugar, rum, orange peel and spices, beating well. Add butter to a medium-hot skillet. Dip bread slices in egg mixture, then dip in plate of crushed corn flakes, turning to coat both sides. Fry in butter until golden brown; turn and brown other side. When done, remove to serving platter, sprinkle with powdered sugar, and serve with Cinnamon-Raisin Sauce (recipe follows).

Cinnamon-Raisin Sauce

In a saucepan, melt butter over medium heat. Blend in flour, stirring constantly 1-2 minutes, until mixture bubbles. Remove pan from heat and gradually whisk in water, then sugar. Return to heat, and cook until thick, and just beginning to boil. Add vanilla, cinnamon and raisins, mixing well. Serve warm over French toast.

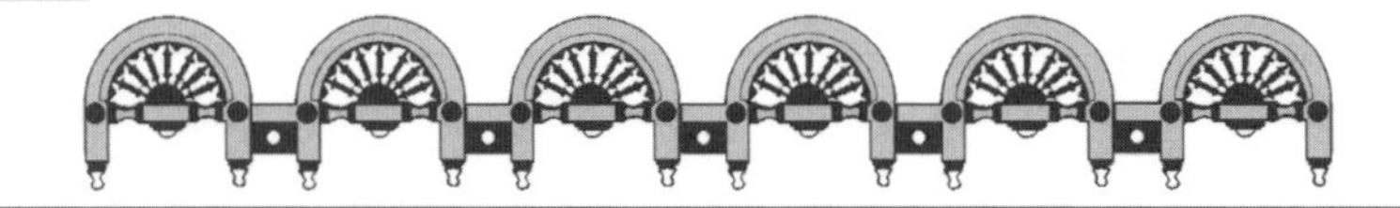

Stuffed French Toast

- 10-12 slices of bread without crust (may substitute cinnamon-raisin bread)
- 8 oz. packages of cream cheese
- 12 eggs
- 5 cups milk
- 1/3 cup maple-flavored syrup
- cinnamon and nutmeg

Cube bread, spread half in greased 9x13" baking dish. Cube cream cheese and place on bread cubes. Top cream cheese layer with remaining bread cubes and set aside.

Combine eggs, milk and maple-flavored syrup, mixing well. Pour egg mixture over bread in baking dish and top with cinnamon and nutmeg. Refrigerate (covered) overnight. In the morning bake at 375° for 45-50 minutes (uncovered), or until done. Serve while warm with additional syrup, or pureed fresh fruit.

Makes 12 servings.

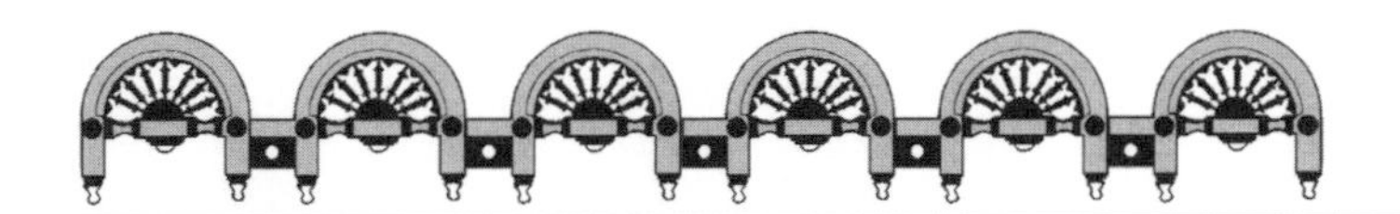

Buttermilk Waffles

- 4 cups flour
- ½ cup packed brown sugar
- 2 t baking soda
- 3 t baking powder
- 1 t cinnamon
- 1 t salt
- 6 eggs, separated (room temperature)
- 4 cups buttermilk
- 1 cup butter (2 sticks), melted
- 2 t vanilla

In large mixing bowl, combine dry ingredients and mix well. In another bowl whisk together egg yolks, buttermilk, butter and vanilla. Add dry ingredients and combine.

Beat egg whites until stiff. Fold into batter.

Serves 10-12.

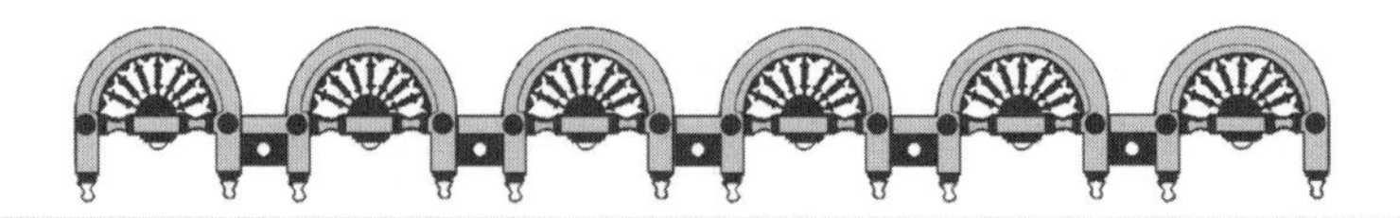

Chocolate Waffles

1 cup whole wheat flour
1 cup flour
1 T sugar
2 t baking powder
1 t baking soda
1/8 t salt
3 eggs, separated
2 cups buttermilk
½ cup butter, melted
½ cup mini chocolate chips

Whisk together dry ingredients, set aside. Beat egg whites to soft peaks and set aside. Blend end yolks, buttermilk and butter in a large bowl. Add dry ingredients. Mix just until moistened. Fold in egg whites and chocolate chips.

Serve these topped with whipped cream and raspberry sauce.

Serves 6.

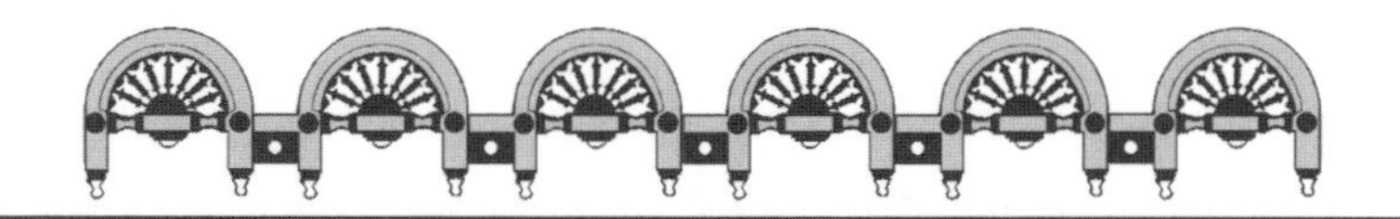

Raised Waffles

¾ cup warm water
1½ T active dry yeast
1⅛ t sugar
2 ½ cups warm water
1⅛ cup powdered milk
¾ cup butter, melted
1⅛ t salt
3 cups flour (all white, all whole wheat or half and half)
3 eggs
½ t baking soda

Dissolve yeast and sugar in warm water for 5 minutes.

Add 2½ cups water, milk, butter, salt and flour and whisk until smooth. Cover and let stand overnight at room temperature. In morning, add eggs and baking soda and stir until well combined.

Top with fresh berries and whipped cream.

Yields 8 servings.

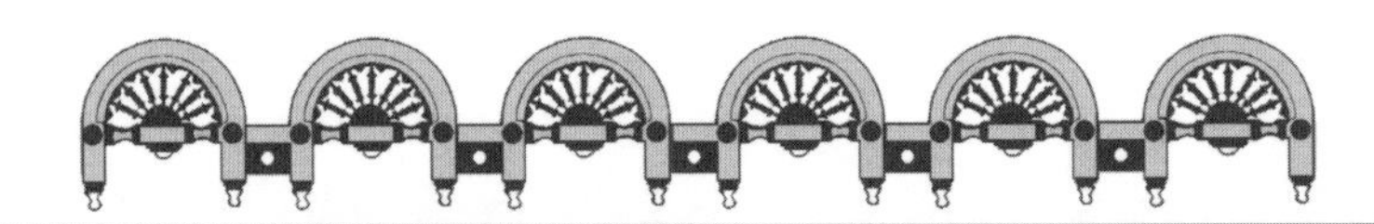

Pumpkin Waffles

2 ¼ cups flour
½ cup brown sugar, packed
4 t baking powder
1 t salt
1 ½ cups pumpkin (canned)
½ to ¾ cup buttermilk
4 eggs
6 T unsalted butter, melted
and cooled
2 t orange zest

Whisk together flour, baking powder, salt and sugar. In a large bowl beat the eggs slightly. Add the buttermilk, butter, orange zest and pumpkin and mix to incorporate. Add the dry ingredients and mix well.

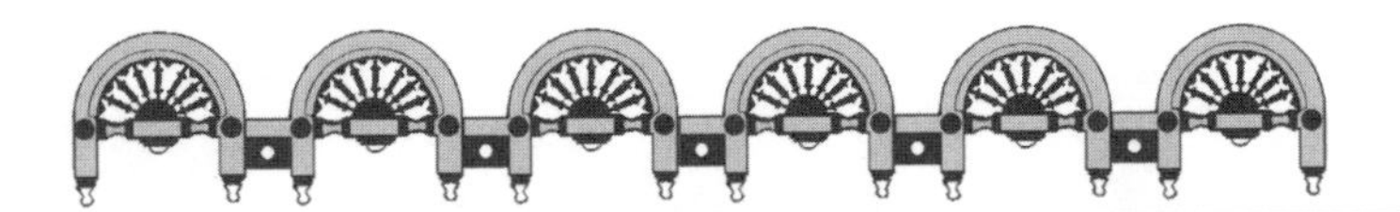

Our Famous Gingerbread Waffles with Honey Apple Cider Sauce

3 cups flour
2 t baking powder
½ t salt
2 t cinnamon
2 t ginger
½ t allspice
4 eggs, separated
½ cup butter, softened
1 cup brown sugar, firmly packed
⅛ cup molasses
1½ cup milk

Honey Apple Cider Sauce
1½ cup apple cider
⅓ cup honey
⅓ cup sugar
1 large Granny Smith apple, peeled and diced
2 T corn starch
⅛ t nutmeg
2 T lemon juice
pinch of salt
1 ½ T unsalted butter

Sift dry ingredients together. Beat egg whites until stiff, but not dry. In a large electric mixer bowl, cream butter until light and fluffy. Add sugar gradually and beat until light and fluffy. Add egg yolks and blend well. Add molasses and blend. Add dry ingredients and milk alternately. Beat until smooth. Fold in egg whites.

Serve with whipped cream and Honey Apple Cider Sauce.

Honey Apple Cider Sauce

Simmer cider, honey and sugar in a saucepan until sugar is dissolved. Add apple. Whisk together cornstarch, nutmeg, lemon juice and salt and add to cider mixture. Simmer for one minute. Add batter to the sauce. Stir until melted and incorporated.

Makes 2½ cups. Serves 6-8.

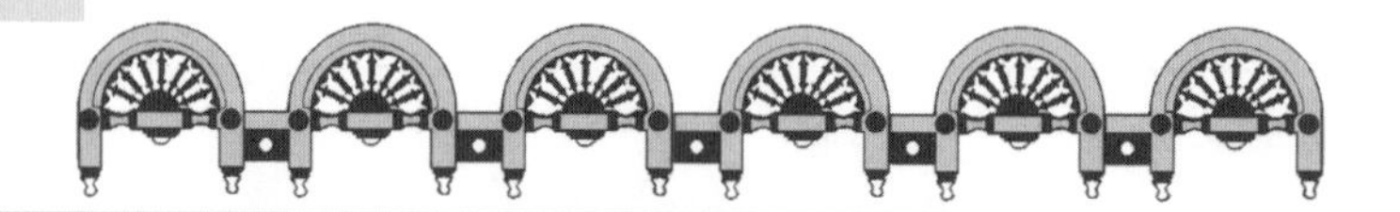

Gingerbread Mansion Buttermilk Pancakes

4 eggs
4 cups buttermilk
½ cups oil
4 cups flour
4 T sugar
4 t baking powder
2 t baking soda
½ t salt

Beat eggs, add oil and buttermilk, mix. Mix dry ingredients thoroughly and beat just until all are combined.

Serves 8-10.

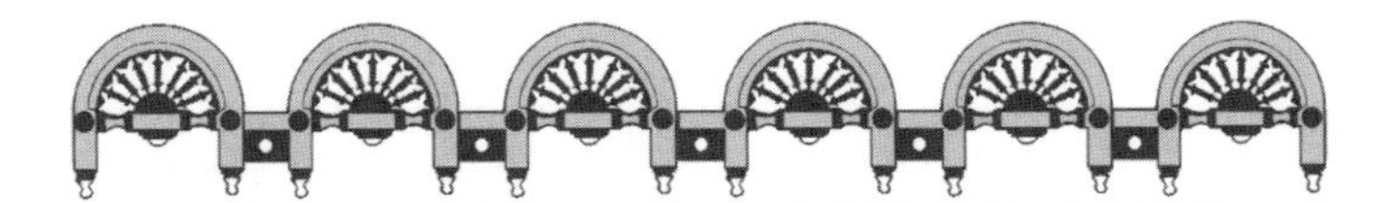

Banana Cream Topping for Buttermilk Pancakes

- 4 ripe bananas, peeled and sliced
- 1 cup apple juice
- 2/3 cup powdered sugar
- 1/4 cup fresh lemon juice
- 1 1/2 cups chilled whipped cream

Combine bananas, apple juice, powdered sugar and lemon juice in medium saucepan over medium heat. Cook until bananas are very soft, about 3 minutes. Using slotted spoon, transfer bananas to food processor. Add 1/3 cup liquid from pan to bananas (discarding remaining liquid). Puree until smooth. Chill until cold.

Whip cream in medium bowl until stiff peaks form. Fold whipped cream into chilled banana puree.

Note: Use the recipe for buttermilk pancakes, placing 6 or 8 thin banana slices on each pancake after pouring batter on to the skillet. When done, top with banana cream and sprinkle with nutmeg.

Makes 5 cups.

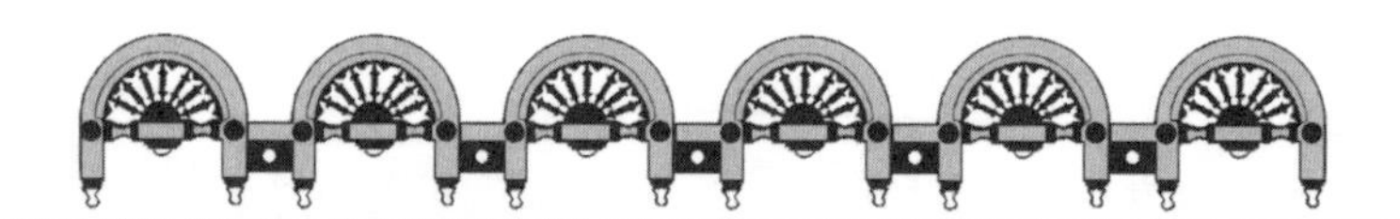

Aebleskiver (Pancake Balls)

Beat eggs until light and fluffy. Add sugar and cream and beat again. Add dry ingredients that have been sifted together and milk.

Cook in aebleskiver pan (monk's pan) that has been greased with butter. Fill each well 2/3 full of batter and put a few raisins or apples in center of each. When browned, turn over with a fork or toothpick and cook until done.

Serve with jam, jelly or syrup.

- 3 eggs
- 3 T sugar
- 1 cup heavy cream
- 2 1/3 cups flour, sifted
- 4 t baking powder
- ½ t cardamon
- ½ t salt
- 1 cup milk
- 1 cup plumped raisins (or pieces of partially cooked apple)

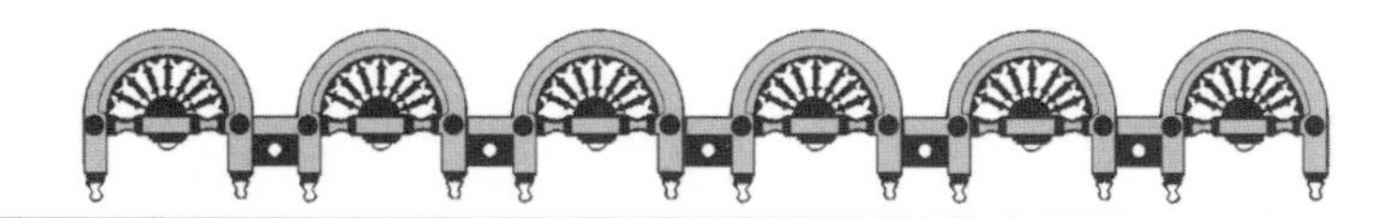

Blintz Casserole

Filling
1 lb. cottage cheese, drained
1 8 oz. cream cheese, softened
2 egg yolks
1 T sugar
1 t vanilla

Batter
1½ cups sour cream
½ cup orange juice
6 eggs
¼ cup butter
1 cup flour
⅓ cup sugar
2 t baking powder
½ t cinnamon

Topping
Sour cream
Fruit preserves

Filling

Using an electric mixer or food processor, mix all ingredients; set aside.

Batter

To make batter: Gradually add all the ingredients in a blender, in the order given. Pour half the batter into a greased 9x13" baking dish. Gently spread the filling over the batter; it will mix a little. Pour the rest of the batter over the filling. Cover and refrigerate overnight.

In the morning, bake at 350°, uncovered for 50-60 minutes. The casserole will be slightly puffed and golden in color. Set on a rack to cool; then cut into squares, top each portion with a dollop of sour cream and preserves and serve immediately.

Serves 8.

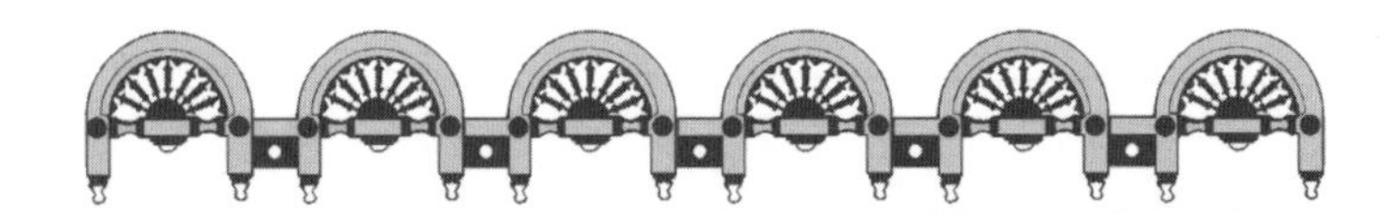

Savory Sausage Souffle

Grease six small ramekin dishes with cooking spray. Fill each dish ½ full with cubed bread. Divide the sausage evenly between the ramekin dishes. Cover with cheese and remaining bread cubes. Lightly beat eggs, add milk and remaining ingredients. Mix well and pour into ramekin dishes, filling almost to the top.

Cover and refrigerate overnight. Bake, uncovered, at 350° for 30 minutes.

Serves 6.

- 3 slices white bread, cubed
- 3 slices whole wheat bread, cubed
- 1 lb. sausage, sauteed with 1 teaspoon fennel or anise, drained
- 1 ½ cups cheddar cheese, shredded
- 6 eggs
- 2¾ cups milk
- 1 t dry mustard
- ¼ t oregano, crushed
- ¼ t basil, crushed
- ¼ t salt
- ⅛ t pepper

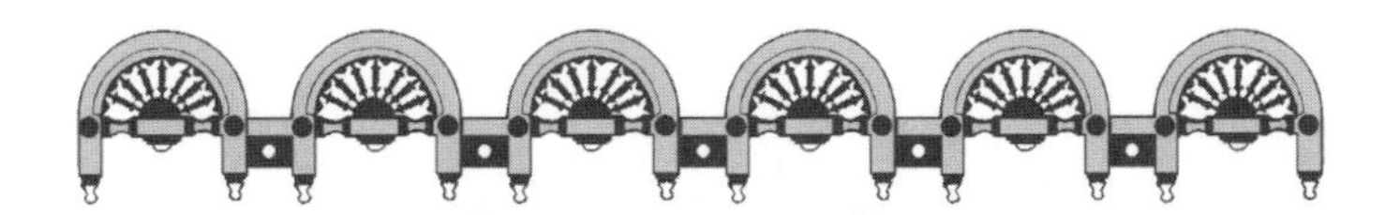

Spicy Eggs and Cheese Souffle

- 1 loaf sliced sourdough french bread
- 1 ½ cups shredded cheddar cheese
- 1 ½ cups shredded jack cheese
- 2 ½ cups cubed cooked ham
- 1 4 oz. can chopped mild green chile peppers
- 12 eggs
- 6 cups milk
- 2 ½ t dry mustard
- chopped green onions
- chopped mushrooms
- dash of Cumin

Grease 12, 8-oz. ramekins. Cut bread into cubes and place enough in a greased 8-oz. ramekin to fill bottom. Sprinkle chile peppers, mushrooms and green onions over bread. Divide chopped ham evenly among the ramekins and top with cheeses.

Beat eggs, add mustard and milk and beat well. Fill ramekins. Sprinkle with paprika; cover and store in refrigerator overnight.

Bake uncovered at 350° for 30 minutes.

Yields 12, 8-oz. servings.

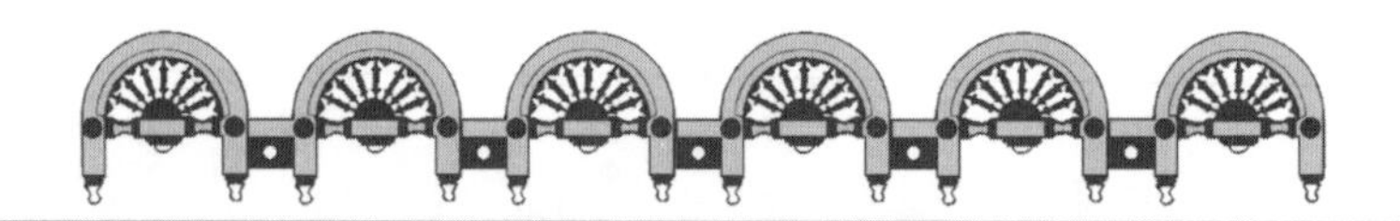

Creamy Scrambled Eggs

2 T butter
½ cup finely chopped shallots
1/3 cup whipping cream
3 oz. cream cheese, cut into small pieces
5 large eggs
salt and pepper
chopped parsley
sauteed mushrooms

In a large frying pan (8 to 10") melt butter over low heat. Add shallots and stir until limp. Add cream and cheese. Stir until cheese is melted. In a bowl, lightly beat eggs with salt and pepper to taste. Pour egg mixture into pan, gently stirring to blend with cream mixture. Cook just until eggs are softly set. Transfer to warm plates and sprinkle with parsley. Spoon sauteed mushrooms along side.

Sauteed Mushrooms

In a 6 to 8" frying pan melt 2 tablespoons butter. Add ½ pound rinsed and drained sliced mushrooms. Cook, stirring over medium-high heat until mushrooms are lightly browned. Add salt to taste.

Makes 4 servings.

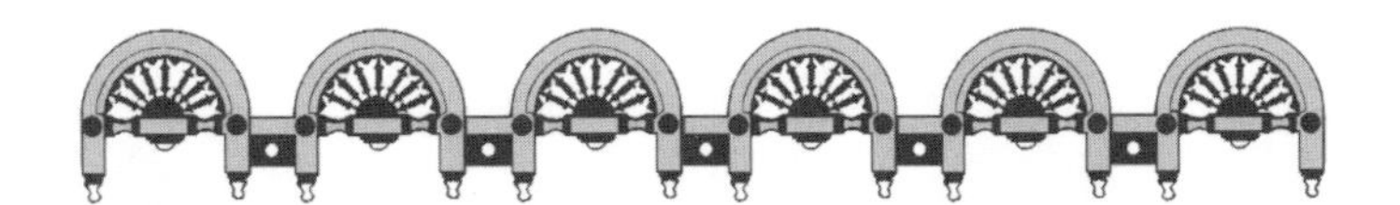

Bacon and Cheese Quiche

1 pie crust recipe
1 9" pie plate
6 slices of bacon fried and cut into pieces
1 bunch green onions, chopped
4-5 large mushrooms, sliced
sharp cheddar cheese, grated

Mixture
3 eggs, slightly beaten
¾ cup mayonnaise
¾ cup half & half
2 t cornstarch

Arrange bacon, green onions and mushrooms on the bottom of a 9" pie shell. Sprinkle the desired amount of grated cheese on top. Fill pie shell with the mixture that has been combined.

Bake in 375° oven for 45 minutes. Cool slightly before cutting. The following ingredients may be substituted or added: chili's, spinach, ham, bell pepper, Swiss cheese, tomatoes.

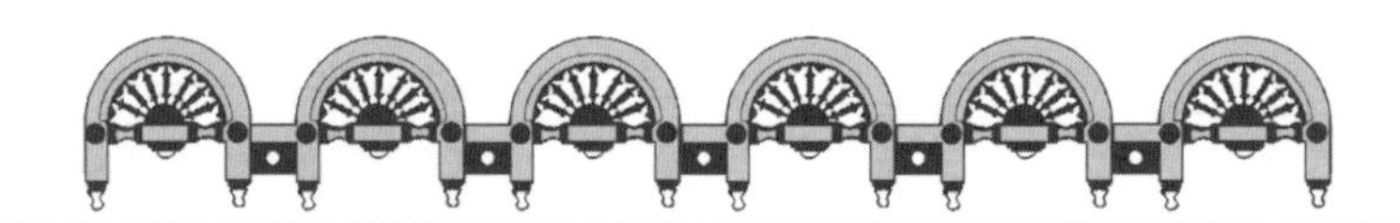

Torta Veneto

1 pkg. frozen puff pastry
½ lb. bulk sausage
1 cup grated sharp cheddar cheese
½ cup parmesan cheese
1 t anise seed
1 medium yellow onion, diced fine
2 cups chicken broth
2 cups vegetable broth
1/3 cup olive oil
½ cup grated swiss cheese
1 cup polenta or cornmeal
1 egg
1 clove garlic (minced)
1 ½ cup fresh spinach, stems removed, washed and coarsely chopped
¼ cup butter
water
additional parmesan cheese
1 12" round pizza pan

About the recipe:

Torta Veneto was created to introduce the Gingerbread Mansion Inn's newest room, the "Veneto Room". Polenta-type cornmeal widely grown in the Veneto region of Italy lends a hearty consistency to this sausage and spinach torta.

Set out puff pastry to thaw (will take about 30-40 minutes). Sprinkle anise seed over sausage and mix well. Add to medium-size frying pan and cook over medium-high heat until done. Drain and reserve. Using the same pan, add olive oil and heat over medium heat. When hot, add chopped onion and saute until transparent and golden. Remove from pan and set aside.

Meanwhile, bring chicken and vegetable broths and minced garlic to a boil in heavy saucepan over high heat. Reduce heat to medium-high and gradually add polenta, stirring constantly with a wire whisk. Continue stirring until polenta thickens and begins to pull away from sides of pan (about 10-15 minutes). Add butter, onion, cheddar and parmesan cheeses, sausage and spinach. Stir to combine then cover to keep warm.

(See next page.)

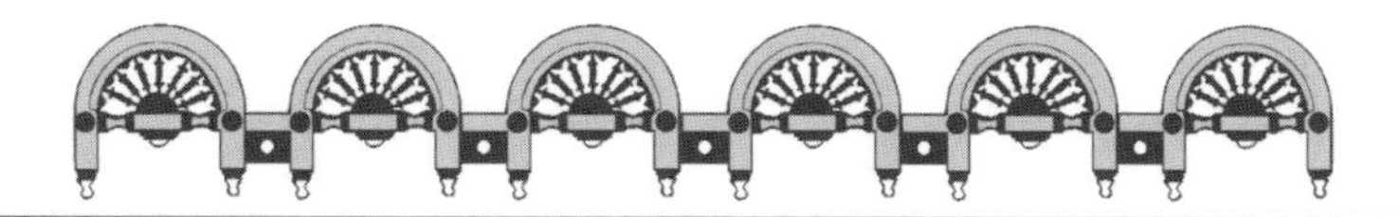

Torta Veneto
(continued)

Gently unfold puff pastry sheets on a floured board. Roll out one sheet to a 14" square, trim to make a 14" round. Roll out second sheet to same size and using the pizza pan as a template, cut out a 12" round. Lay the first round in the pan. Spread with the polenta mixture to within 1½" of sides. Wet outside 1½" edge with a little water. Sprinkle top of polenta mixture with Swiss cheese and additional parmesan cheese.

Put the second pastry sheet on top and press around the edges to seal. Then roll bottom pastry sheet inward all the way around and crimp to seal completely. Cut slits in top to allow steam to escape. Brush with beaten egg mixed with a little water and sprinkle lightly with parmesan cheese.

Bake in 350° oven for 35-40 minutes until top is golden brown. Remove from oven; transfer to cutting board. Cut into wedges and serve.

Serves 10-12 people.

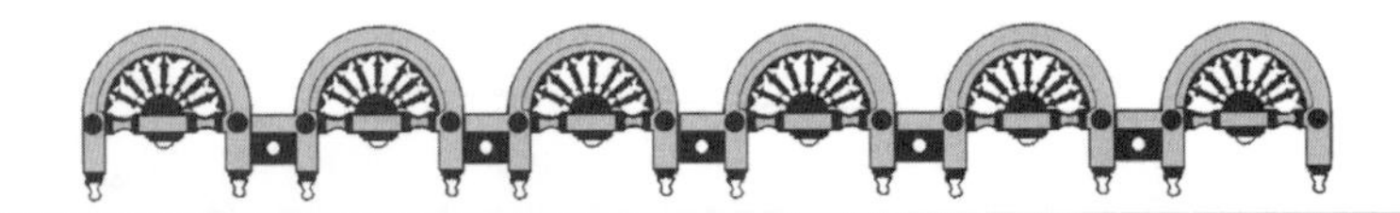

Very Good

Eggs Florentine with Creamy Cheese Sauce

Eggs Florentine

Beat eggs slightly; add cheeses and butter and mix well. Stir in spinach and nutmeg; pout into 12 greased, 8-oz. ramekins or 9x11" casserole dish. Bake at 350° for 30-45 minutes, or until toothpick inserted in center comes out clean. Serve with creamy cheese sauce.

Creamy Cheese Sauce

Melt butter, stir in flour and cook while stirring for several minutes. Add milk, stirring constantly until sauce begins to thicken and bubble. Stir in cheese and seasonings, and cook until cheese is melted.

Yields 12.

Eggs Florentine

12 eggs
4 T butter, softened
1 pint cottage cheese
2 10 oz. pkgs. frozen chopped spinach, thawed and drained
8 oz. Swiss cheese, grated
8 oz. Feta cheese, cubed
1 t nutmeg

Creamy Cheese Sauce

2 T butter
3 T flour
2 cups milk
2 cups grated Jack cheese
½ t salt
¼ t dry mustard
¼ t cayenne pepper

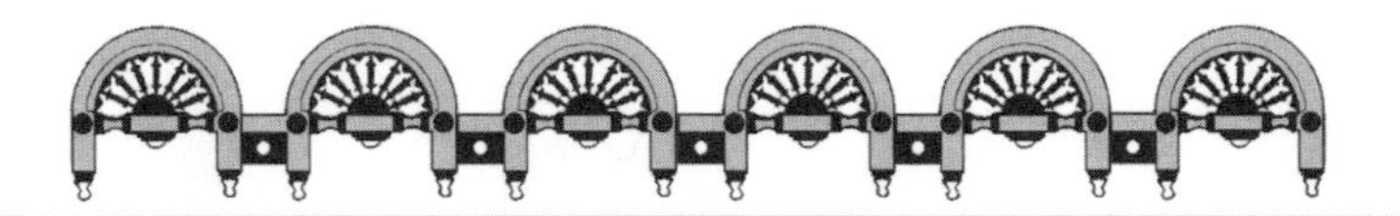

Fancy Egg Scramble

½ cup butter
1 cup chopped ham
½ cup chopped green onion
½ cup chopped green pepper
½ cup chopped mushrooms
1 cup grated cheddar cheese
12 eggs, beaten
3 T flour
½ t salt
$^1/_8$ t pepper
2 cups milk
$^1/_8$ t paprika
3 slices white bread, trimmed and cubed

This must be assembled the night before, refrigerated and baked in the morning.

Saute the ham, onions, peppers and mushrooms in 3 tablespoons of butter. Add the beaten eggs and scramble. Remove from heat and put into a large mixing bowl.

In a saucepan using low heat, melt 3 tablespoons butter; blend in the flour. Add the milk and stir until bubbly. Add the cheese, stirring until melted. Remove from heat and pour into the scrambled egg mixture. Stir until well combined and then spoon into a greased 11x7x2" baking dish. Distribute the bread cubes evenly over the top of the eggs. Melt the remaining 2 tablespoons butter and drizzle over the bread cubes. Sprinkle with paprika. Cover and refrigerate overnight.

Remove from the refrigerator 45 minutes before baking. Bake uncovered at 350° for 30-40 minutes. Remove from oven, cut into squares and serve with hot biscuits.

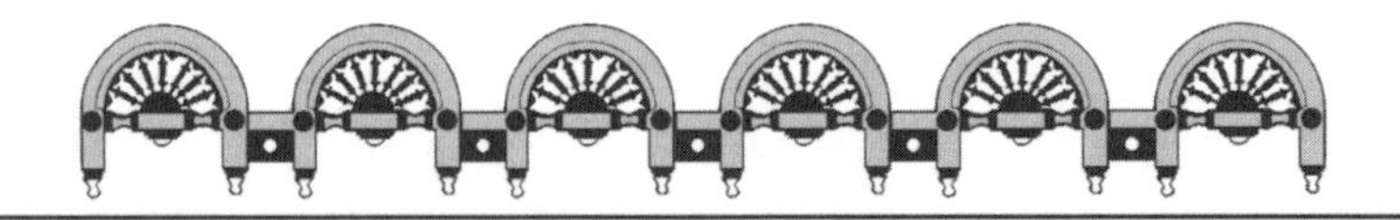

Gingerbread Mansion Inn Special Eggs Benedict with Creamy Hollandaise Sauce

Eggs Benedict

Grease 12, 8-oz. ramekins; set aside. Cube English muffins and place enough in each ramekin to fill half way. Sprinkle muffins with a small handful of cheese. Place a slice of Canadian bacon on next and top with more cheese.

Beat eggs slightly, add milk and peppers to taste. Divide among ramekins. Cover and place in refrigerator overnight.

Bake uncovered at 350° for 30 minutes. Spoon creamy hollandaise sauce on top and sprinkle with paprika before serving.

Creamy Hollandaise Sauce

Melt butter to low boiling point. Place all other ingredients in blender and blend at low speed until mixed. Slowly pour in melted butter and blend 10 seconds or until thick and creamy.

Yields 12, 8-oz. servings.

Eggs Benedict
1 pkg. English muffins
12 eggs
8 oz. grated Swiss cheese
Cayenne pepper, to taste
6 cups milk
Pepper, to taste
12 slices Canadian bacon

Creamy Hollandaise Sauce
¼ lb. butter
1 T sherry
1 T lemon juice
3 dashes Cayenne pepper
3 egg yolks

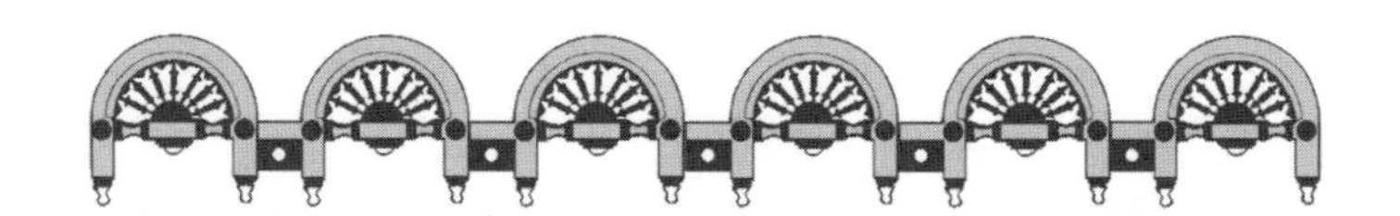

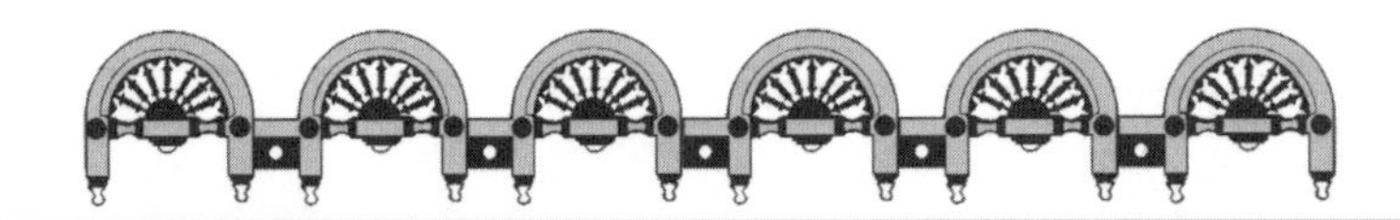

Sumptuous Sauces & Side Dishes

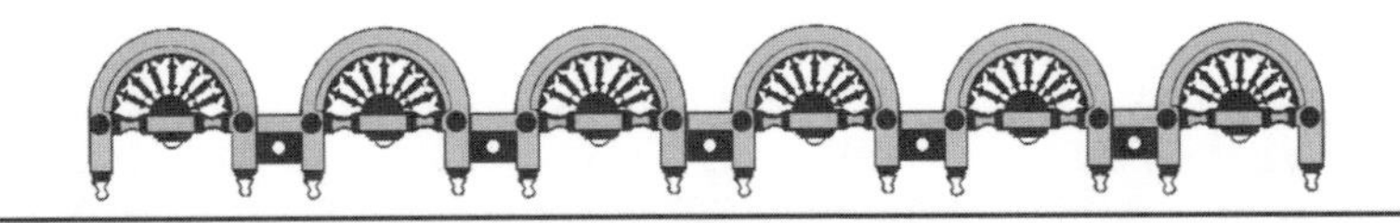

Maple Cream

¾ cup whipping cream
½ cup maple syrup

This flavored whipped cream is good over buttermilk pancakes or waffles, with sliced bananas and a sprinkle of nutmeg.

Whip cream just until it begins to thicken. With the beaters running, pour in the syrup and continue beating until mixture is thick.

Makes 2 cups.

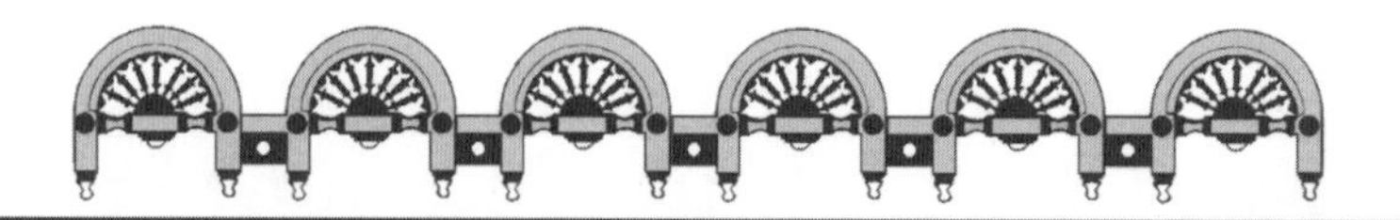

Orange Cream Fruit Topping

Combine sugar and cream cheese and beat until smooth and fluffy. Add remaining ingredients.

Serve over mixed fresh fruit.

¼ cup confectioners sugar
8 oz. cream cheese, softened
⅓ cup orange juice
2 t grated orange peel
1 T orange flavored liqueur

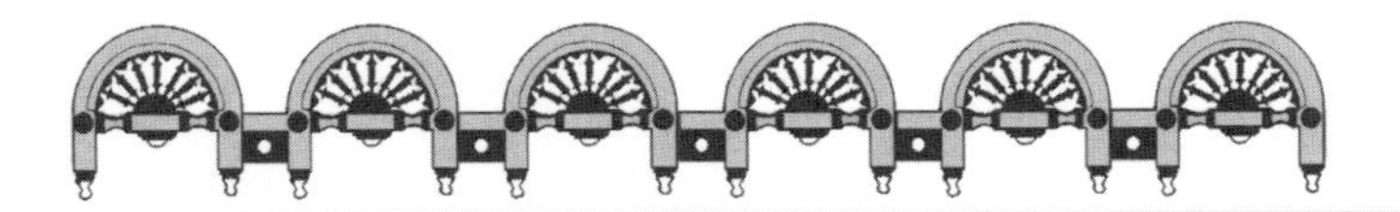

Cream Anglaise

- 2 cups whole milk
- 5 egg yolks, slightly beaten
- 2/3 cup sugar
- 1/8 t salt
- 1 t vanilla

Scald milk in double boiler. Slowly stir in yolks, sugar and salt. Stir until thickened, 5 to 10 minutes. Remove from heat. As mixture cools, beat to release steam. When cool, add vanilla. A tasty topping for fresh seasonal berries such as raspberries, strawberries or blackberries.

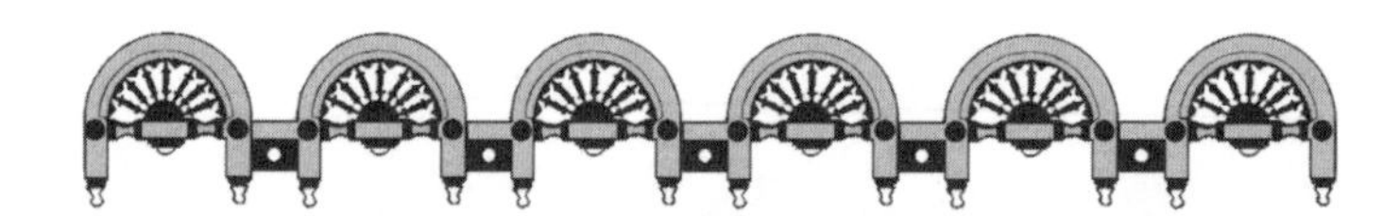

Cinnamon Sauce

Melt butter in medium sized saucepan. Add flour and stir to incorporate, cooking over medium heat until bubbly, about 1 minute. Slowly whisk in water and sugar and cook over medium heat until thickened. Add vanilla and cinnamon.

May be used as a topping for stuffed French toast, pancakes or used over warm cinnamon rolls.

2 T butter
2 T flour
1 cup water
1 cup sugar
1 t vanilla
1 t cinnamon

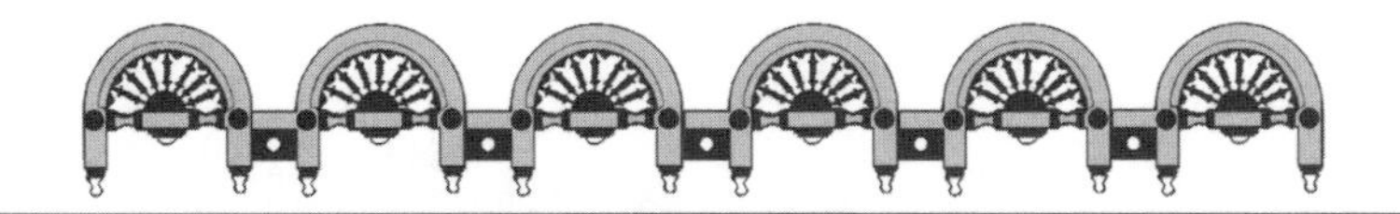

Honey Cream Fruit Sauce

1 pint sour cream
½ cup honey
¼ cup orange

Whisk ingredients together until smooth. Chill. A wonderful topping for fresh fruit.

Makes 3 cups.

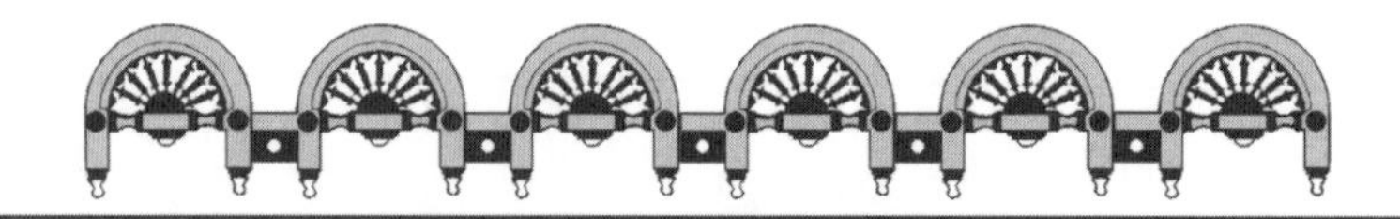

Orange Apricot Grand Marnier Sauce

Mix all ingredients and heat before serving.

Yields 1½ cups (6 servings).

½ cup orange marmalade
¼ cup fresh orange juice
¾ cup apricot puree
2 T Grand Marnier Liqueur

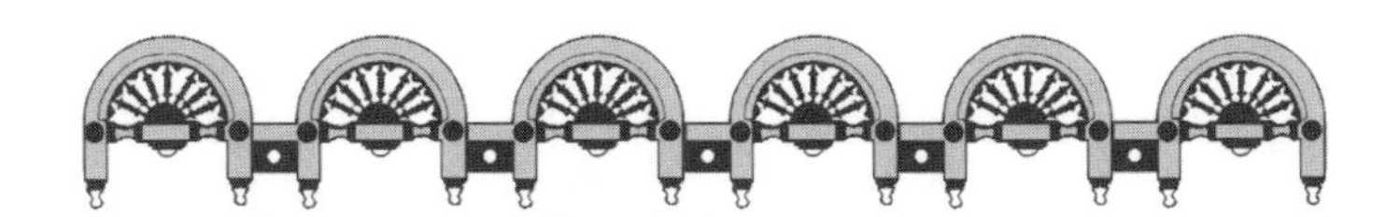

Orange Sauce

2 t butter
1½ cup honey
2 T grated orange rind
½ cup orange juice
2 t orange extract
Fresh peaches
Whipped cream

In a saucepan, melt butter with honey. Remove from heat and stir in orange zest, juice and extract. Drizzle warm over French toast. Add peach slices and top with whipped cream.

Yields 2 cups.

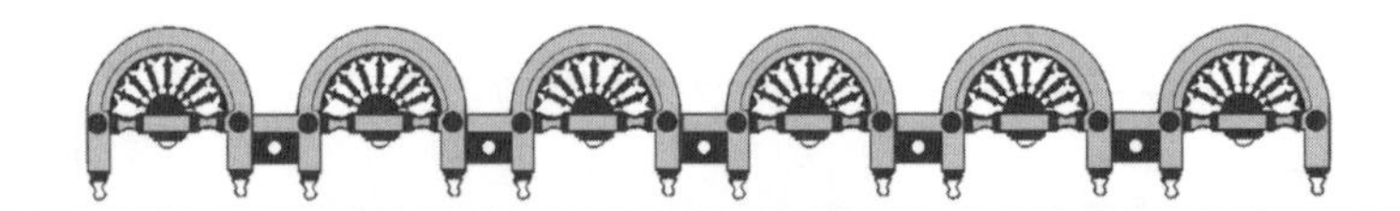

Peach Apricot Sauce

In blender, puree peaches with syrup until smooth. Pour into saucepan and stir in preserves and liqueur. Cook until thickened. Keep warm until ready to use.

Yields 6-8 servings.

- 1 6 oz. can peaches in syrup
- ¾ cup apricot preserves (or jam)
- 3 T Curacao Liqueur

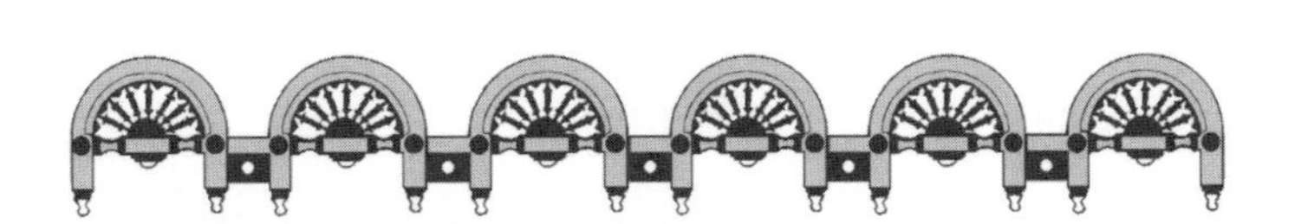

Baked Peaches a la Raspberry Sauce

6 medium peaches
raspberry jam
cream

Preheat oven to 350°. Wash peaches and slice thin piece off top of peach. Remove pit and stuff cavity with raspberry jam. Place peaches in shallow greased dish. Bake 30-40 minutes, cool. Serve chilled in pool of cream.

Serves 6.

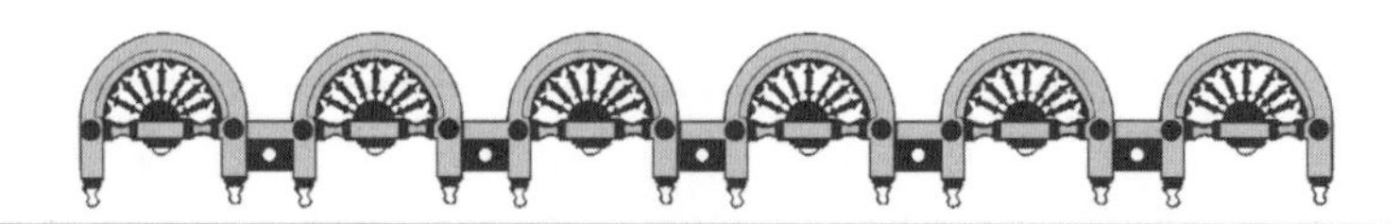

Blueberry Sauce for French Toast

Combine water, sugar and cornstarch with 1 cup blueberries and cook until sauce thickens, stirring frequently. Mix in 1 more cup blueberries and butter. Cook until blueberries are heated through.

Serves 12.

1 cup water
1 cup sugar
2 T cornstarch
2 cups blueberries*
1 T butter

*fresh or frozen raspberries may be used

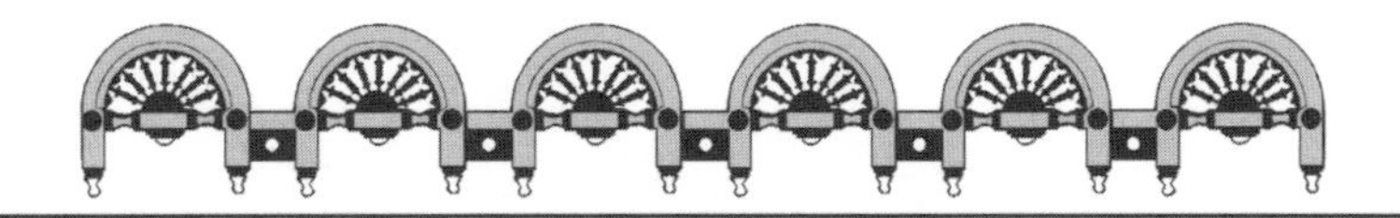

Raspberry-Framboise Cream

½ cup raspberry jam
½ cup Raspberry Liqueur
1 cup heavy cream

Bring jam and liqueur to a slow simmer. Cool and refrigerate.

Whip cream until stiff. Stir desired amount of syrup into whipped cream and serve over fresh fruit compote.

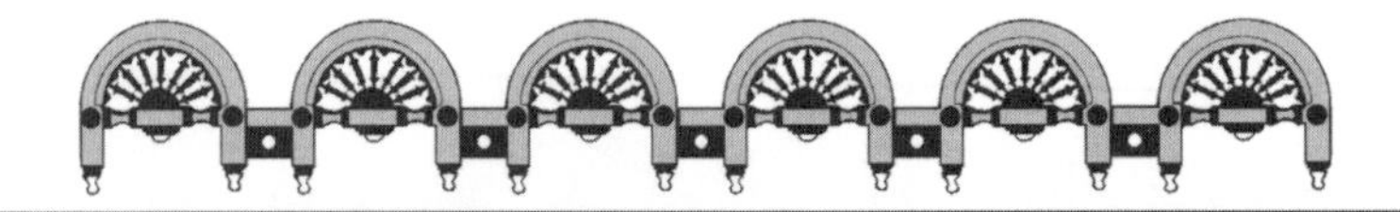

Breakfast Potatoes

6 medium red new potatoes
3 green onions
½ red bell pepper
6 slices bacon
ground cumin (to taste)
turmeric (to taste)
salt and pepper (to taste)

Parboil new red potatoes with skins until just barely done (do NOT overcook). This is best done the day or night before serving. Cover and refrigerate.

Cube potatoes and set aside; chop onion and bell pepper coarsely. Fry bacon in large skillet until crisp; drain on paper towel. Saute onion and bell pepper in bacon drippings until tender; add potatoes and cumin, turmeric, salt and pepper to taste, tossing potatoes to coat. Cook several minutes while continuing to toss. Add bacon that has been crumbled, and pour into 9x13" baking dish. Cover and bake at 300° for 30 minutes.

Yield 6-8 servings.

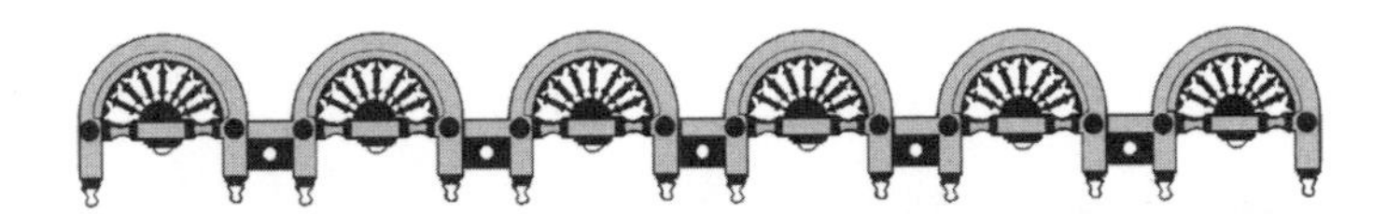

Bacon Wrapped Prunes

pitted, moist, soft prunes
bacon

Wrap prunes in a 1/3 slice of bacon. Secure with toothpick. Arrange on a rack that has been placed on a jelly roll pan and cook in a 375° oven until the bacon is crisp. Turn once during baking. Serve hot.

Allow 2-4 prunes per person and be careful—the prunes are hot!

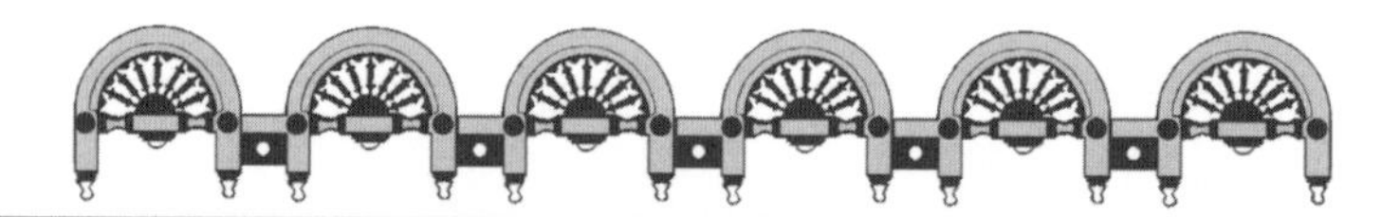

Baked Polenta

4 cups chicken broth
1 cup polenta
1 clove garlic
4 T butter
¼ cup each cheddar and parmesan cheese
additional butter for topping
additional parmesan cheese for topping

Mince garlic and put in a large pan with the chicken broth. Bring to a boil on high heat. Gradually add polenta while stirring broth. Reduce heat and boil gently, stirring constantly until polenta becomes thick and pulls away from sides of pan (about 20-30 minutes). When thick, add butter and cheeses and stir well to combine.

Pour mixture into greased 5x9" loaf pan. When cool, cover and refrigerate overnight.

To serve, remove from pan and slice ¾ inch thick and place overlapping slices in greased shallow casserole. Pour melted butter over top and sprinkle with parmesan cheese. Bake uncovered at 350° for 30 minutes. Serve hot. An excellent side dish for breakfast or dinner.

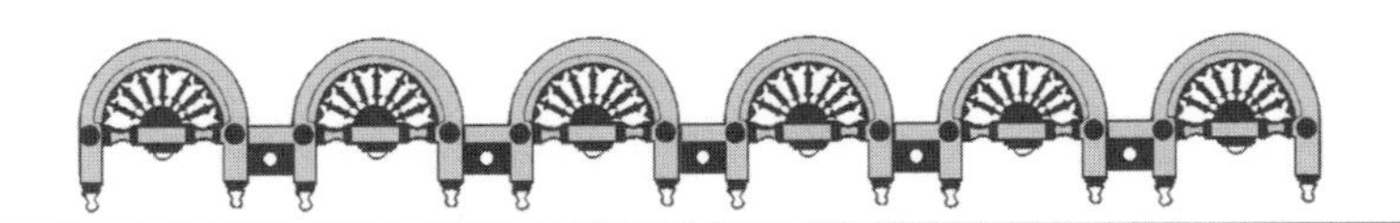

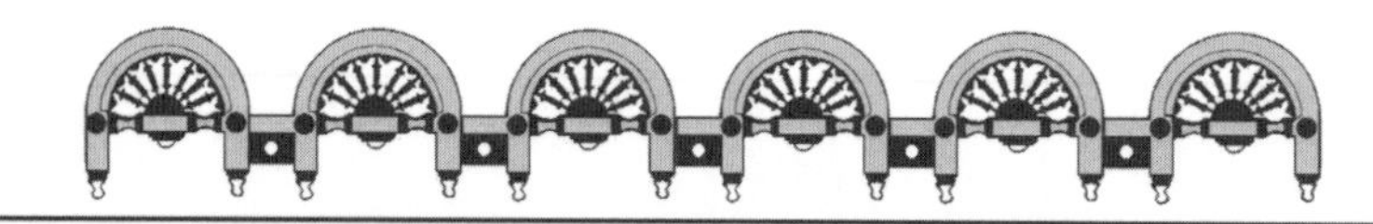

Afternoon Tea

Sweet Confections: Cookies, Tarts, Cakes, Pastries, Scones, Tea Breads

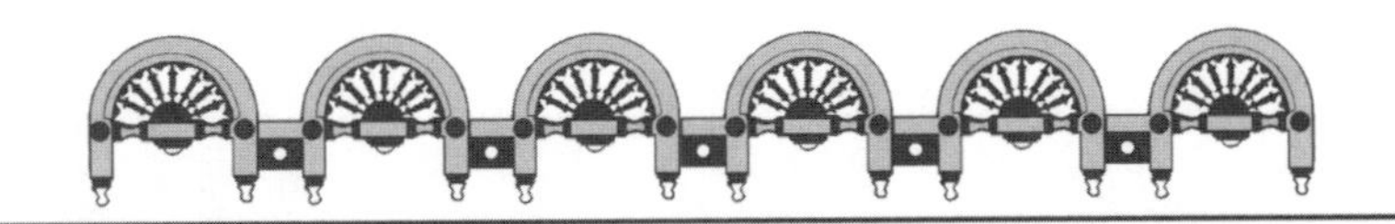

Chocolate Dipped Pecan Shortbread

- 2½ cups flour
- ¾ cup confectioner's sugar
- ½ cup cornstarch
- 1 cup pecans, finely chopped
- 1½ cup butter
- 1-oz. square semi-sweet chocolate

Preheat oven to 325°

In a large bowl, with fork, combine flour, sugar, cornstarch and pecans. With knife, cut butter into small pieces and add to flour mixture. With hands, knead all ingredients until well blended and mixture holds together.

Pat dough evenly into 9x13" baking dish. Bake for 35-40 minutes until golden. With sharp knife immediately cut shortbread lengthwise into 3 strips, then cut each strip crosswise into 12 pieces. Cool in dish or on wire rack. When cold, carefully remove cookies from baking dish.

Melt chocolate in microwave or a small saucepan until smooth. Dip one corner of each cookie in chocolate and place on wax paper-lined tray until set. Store in airtight container. Makes 3 dozen cookies.

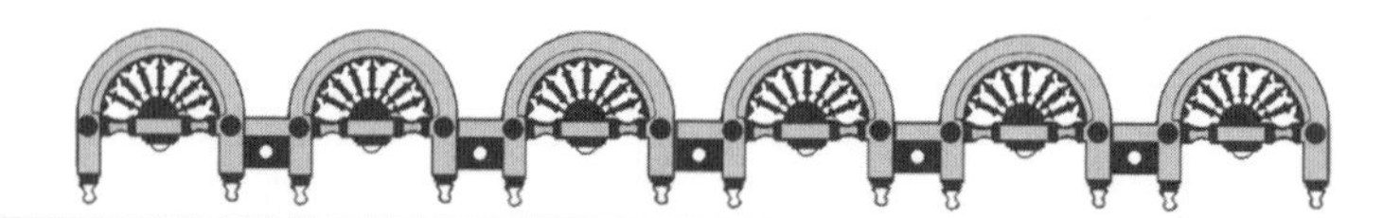

Classic Shortbread

In a large bowl of electric mixer, beat butter until fluffy. Stir together flour, cornstarch, confectioner's sugar, salt and add to butter. Beat at low speed, scraping the sides of the bowl until well combined.

Form dough into a ball. Roll out on an ungreased baking sheet to make a 10" round. Using a 4" dish or saucer or a pattern, with the point of a knife score a 4" round in the center of the dough. Remove dish or saucer and score the 4" center into 4 wedges and the outer circle into 12 pieces. Press tines of fork into edge of round to crimp the edges. Sprinkle granulated sugar over shortbread dough.

Bake 18-20 minutes or until firm and edges begin to brown in a 325° oven.

¾ cups unsalted butter, softened
2¼ cups flour
¼ cup cornstarch
¼ cup confectioner's sugar
¼ t salt
½ t granulated sugar

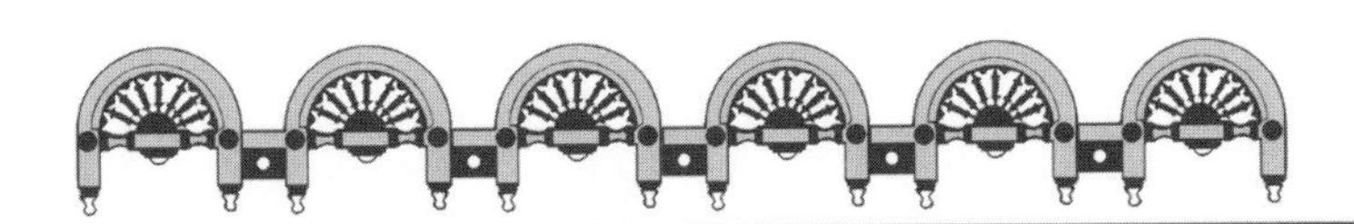

Kringler

(Danish Pretzel Cookie)

1 lb. butter, softened
5½ cups flour
3 egg yolks, slightly beaten
10 T cream
3 egg whites
1 cup sugar

Cream butter and flour; mix egg yolks with cream, then incorporate into butter mixture, blending well. Form into ball, wrap and chill for 30 minutes to 1 hour.

Divide dough into thirds. Roll each section into a 9x14" rectangle, 1/8" thick. Brush top with egg whites that have been beaten slightly. Using a crinkle-cut pastry roller (or pizza cutter), cut strips out of the rectangle, ½" wide by 9 inches long. Twist each strip into pretzel shape and turn egg white-side down into a plate of sugar. Turn right-side up and place on an ungreased baking sheet. Bake at 375° 8-10 minutes, or until lightly browned. Cool on wire rack and store in an airtight container.

Yield: 9 dozen cookies.

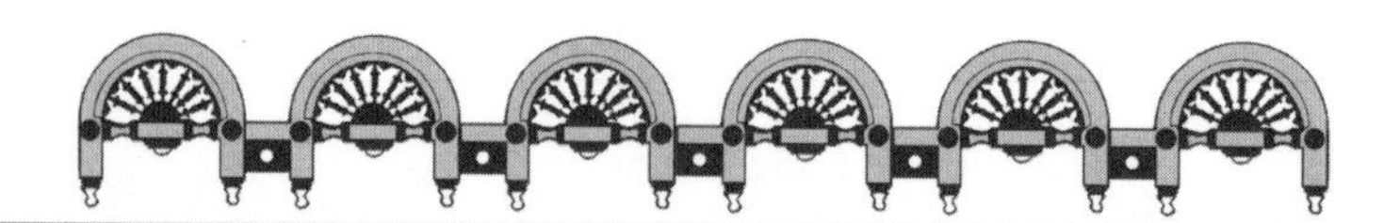

Mexican Wedding Cakes

- 1 cup butter
- 3/4 cup powdered sugar
- 2/3 cup finely chopped nuts
- 2 t vanilla
- 2 3/4 cup cake flour

Cream butter and sugar. Add vanilla, flour and nuts. Roll into 1" balls and bake on greased sheet at 350° for 15 minutes.

When cool, roll in powdered sugar and store in airtight container.

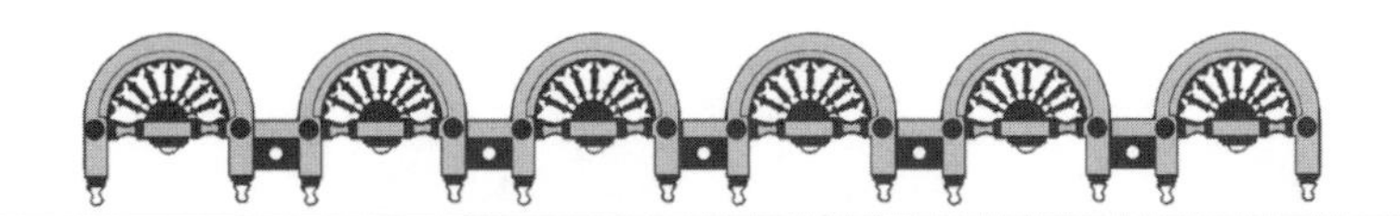

Gingerbread Mansion's Spiced Nut Cookies

- 1 cup butter softened
- 1 cup brown sugar
- 1 cup white sugar
- 3 eggs beaten
- 1 cup walnuts, chopped
- 4 cups flour
- 1 t cinnamon
- ½ t cloves
- ½ t nutmeg
- 1 t soda
- 1 t salt

Sift together flour, cinnamon, cloves, nutmeg, soda and salt.

Cream butter and sugars. Add eggs and cream well. Add nuts then dry ingredients. Shape into log type rolls (5). Wrap in waxed paper and chill overnight. Slice ¼" thick and bake on ungreased cookie sheet for 12 minutes or until lightly browned.

Bake in oven at 350°.

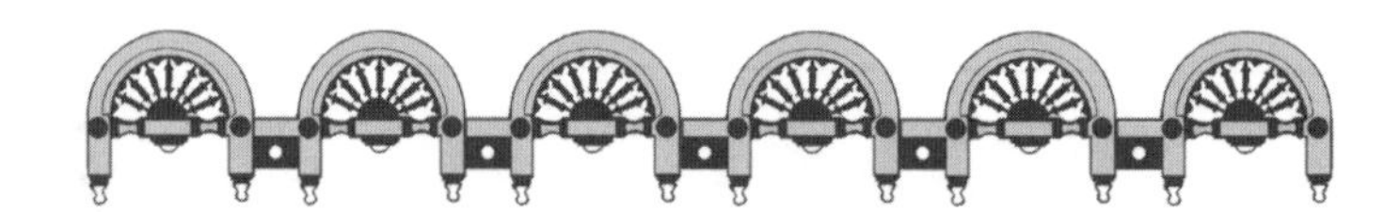

Danish Coconut Butter Cookies

- 2 cups butter, softened
- 1 cup sugar
- 4 cups flour
- 1 cup chopped coconut

Cream butter well. Add sugar gradually and cream well. Add flour then coconut and combine thoroughly. Roll into log type rolls 1½ to 1¾ inches thick and wrap in waxed paper and chill overnight.

Cut into 1/3" thick slices and bake on ungreased sheet for 18 minutes or until lightly browned around edges. Heat oven at 350°.

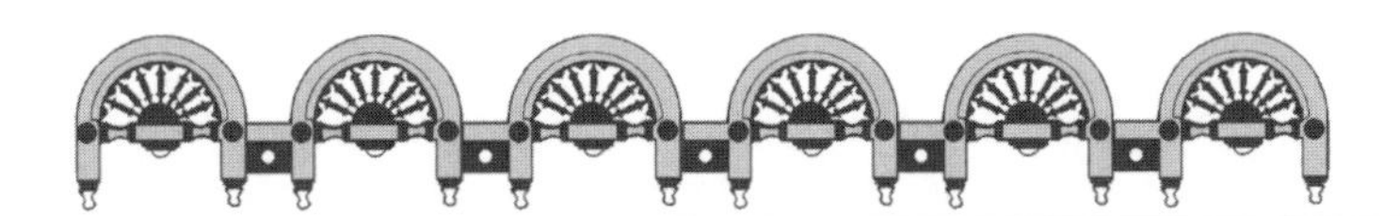

Coconut Macaroons

- ¾ cup water
- 3 cups sugar
- 12 egg whites
- 1½ cup sugar
- 1 t vanilla
- 1 t salt
- 1½ cup shredded coconut

In small saucepan combine water and 3 cups sugar. Bring to boil over medium heat. Brush sides of pan occasionally with water to prevent crystallization. Cook to 242° on candy thermometer. Remove from heat. While sugar is cooking,. beat egg whites until frothy gradually beat in 1½ cups sugar on low until stiff peaks form. Gradually beat in hot sugar mixture. Add vanilla and salt when cool. Gently fold in coconut, scoop dough into balls and place on insulated baking sheet lined with parchment paper. Put a section of maraschino cherry on top of each one before baking. Bake 15 minutes or until golden. at 350°. Store in airtight container.

Makes 3 dozen cookies.

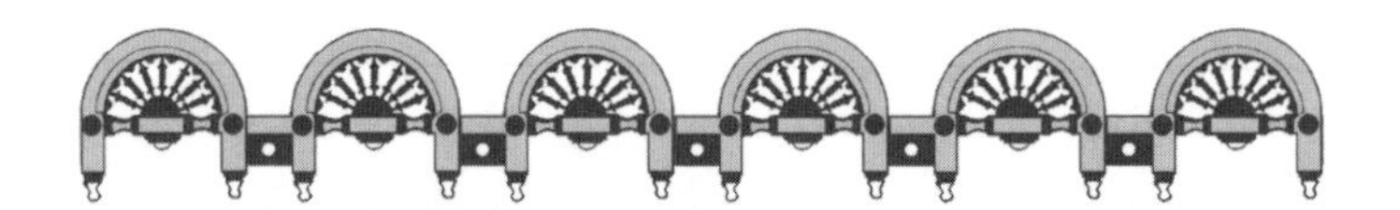

Sachertorte Cookies

Mix together 1 cup butter and all the pudding mix until light and fluffy. Add egg and flour and blend well. Shape dough into 1" balls. Roll in sugar and place 2 inches apart on an ungreased cookie sheet. Make an indentation in the center of each cookie with your finger. Fill each indentation with preserves and bake in a 325° oven for 15 to 18 minutes.

In a saucepan or microwave, melt chocolate chips and 3 tablespoons butter. Stir until smooth. Drizzle over cooled cookies. When set, store in an airtight container.

Makes 4 dozen cookies.

- 1 cup unsalted butter, softened
- 1 4½ oz. package instant chocolate pudding
- 1 egg
- 2 cups flour
- 3 T sugar
- ½ cup apricot or raspberry preserves
- ½ cup semi-sweet chocolate chips
- 3 T butter

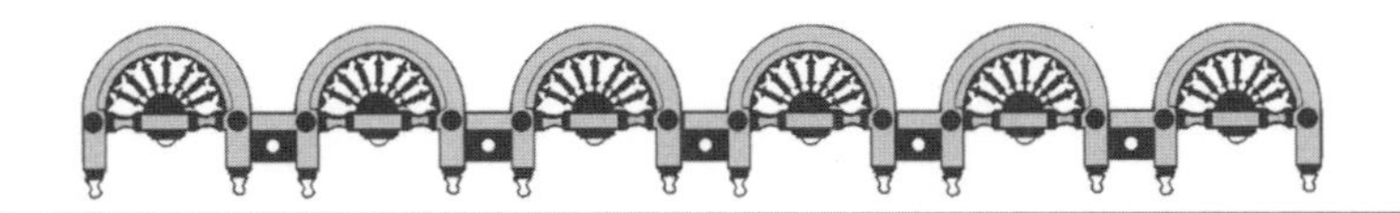

Chocolate Pixies

¼ cup butter
4 1 oz. squares unsweetened
  baking chocolate
2 cups flour
2 cups sugar
4 eggs
2 t baking powder
½ t salt
½ cup chopped walnuts or
  pecans
confectioner's sugar

In a medium saucepan melt butter and chocolate over low heat until melted and smooth, stirring occasionally. Cool completely. In a large mixer bowl combine melted chocolate mixture, 1 cup flour and all remaining ingredients except nuts and confectioner's sugar. Beat at medium speed, scraping bowl often until well-mixed, 2-3 minutes. By hand, stir in remaining flour and nuts. Cover and refrigerate until firm (2 hours).

Shape dough into 1" balls, roll in confectioner's sugar. Place 2 inches apart on a greased baking sheet. Bake in 300°oven for 12-15 minutes.

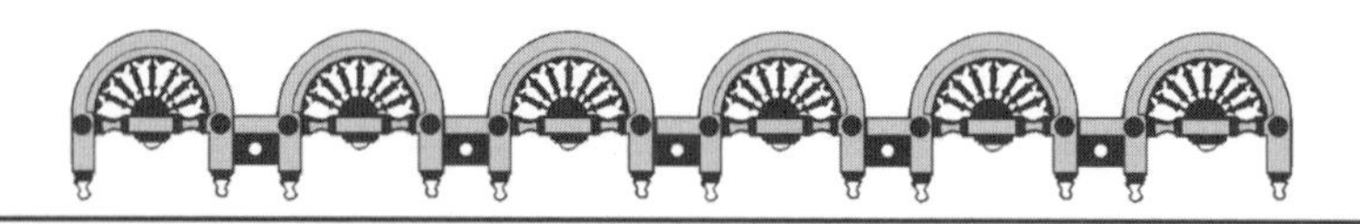

Nut Horn Cookies

Beat 1 cup butter for 30 seconds. Add 2 tablespoons sugar and beat until light and fluffy, about 3 minutes. Beat in sour cream and egg yolk. Combine 1½ cups flour and 1/8 teaspoon salt. Add to beaten mixture. Stir in remaining flour. cover and chill.

Combine nuts, ½ cup sugar, ¼ cup butter and cinnamon. Working with ¼ of the dough at a time, on a lightly floured surface roll to a 10" circle. Spread ¼ of the nut mixture over circle. Cut circle into 12 wedges. Roll up each wedge starting at the wide end. Place on ungreased baking sheet and bake a 350° for 25 minutes. Repeat with remaining dough. Cool on a wire rack. Roll in confectioner's sugar. Store in an airtight container.

- 1 cup butter, softened
- 2 T sugar
- 8 oz. sour cream
- 1 egg yolk
- 2 cups flour
- 1 cup finely chopped walnuts or pecans
- ½ cup sugar
- ¼ cup butter, softened
- 1½ t cinnamon
- confectioner's sugar for coating cookies

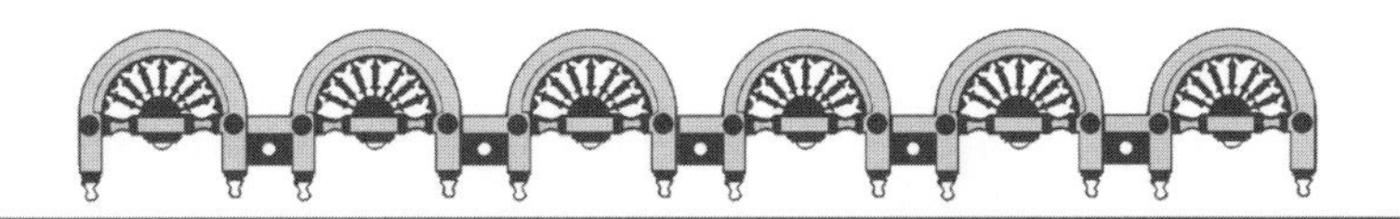

Currant Cookies

1 cup butter
1 cup sugar
3 eggs
3 cups flour
2 t baking powder
1 t salt
1 cup currants
1 cup nuts, finely chopped
(pecans or walnuts)
Additional sugar for topping

Cream butter and sugar. Add eggs one at a time beating well after each addition. Add flour that has been sifted with baking powder and salt. Spread dough in a 10x15" well-greased jelly roll pan. Cover top with currants and nuts and sprinkle with sugar.

Bake in 375° oven for 30 minutes or until lightly browned. While still slightly warm cut into desired shapes.

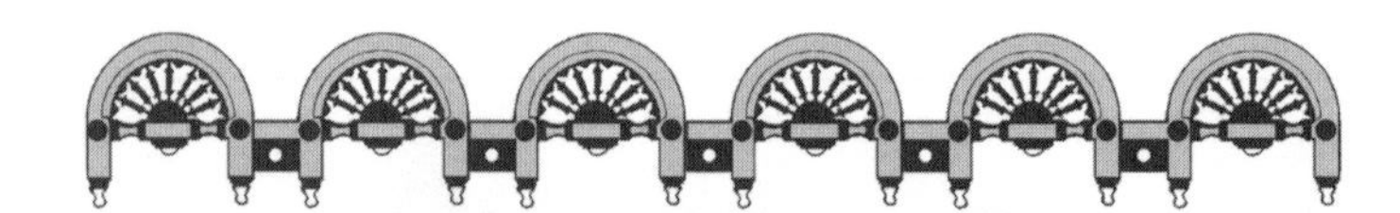

Chocolate Rum Cookies

Sift together flour, cocoa, baking powder and salt. Beat butter and sugar until fluffy. Beat in rum then eggs one at a time, blending well after each addition. Beat in flour mixture. Cover and chill for 1 hour. Roll dough into 1" round balls and bake on a greased sheet at 325° for 15 minutes. Cool on rack. Store in an airtight container.

3 cups flour
1 ½ cups cocoa
1 T baking powder
½ t salt
3 cubes unsalted butter
2 cups sugar
2 T rum
2 eggs, large

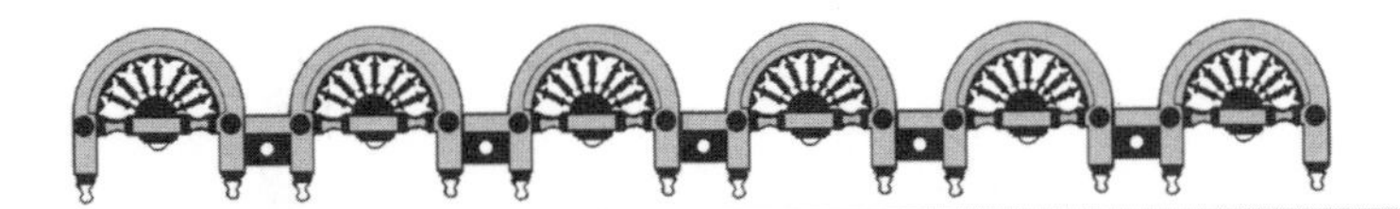

Grandma's Very Good Cookies

1 cup brown sugar
1 cup white sugar
1 cup butter, softened
1 cup margarine
3 eggs
4 cups flour
1 t soda
¼ t salt
1 t nutmeg

Combine flour, soda, salt and nutmeg. Cream butter, margarine and sugars until light and fluffy. Add eggs and beat until well combined. Add flour and beat. Drop by teaspoons full on a greased sheet and flatten with the bottom of a glass that has been dipped in flour. Bake at 325° until lightly browned.

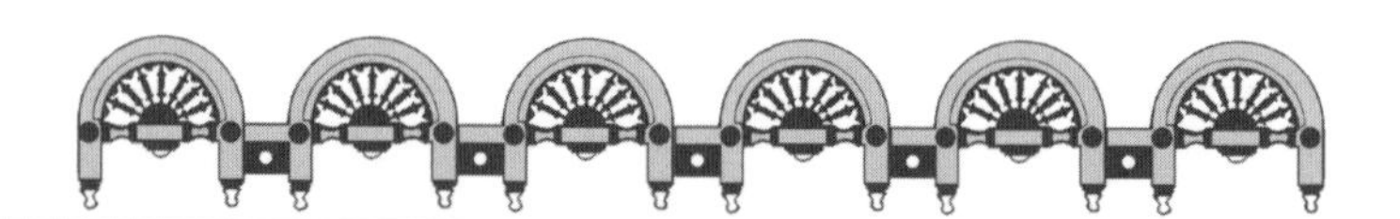

Portuguese Wine Cookies

Sift flour, baking powder, soda and salt. Cream butter and sugar. Add eggs, Mix well. Add wine and mix. Slowly mix in flour mixture and beat until combined. Drop by teaspoons full on greased sheet and bake for 12-15 minutes or until lightly browned around the edge. 325°.

5 cups flour
1½ cups sugar
3 eggs-slightly beaten
½ cup wine (dry white)
1 t baking soda
1 t baking powder
½ t salt
1 cup butter, softened

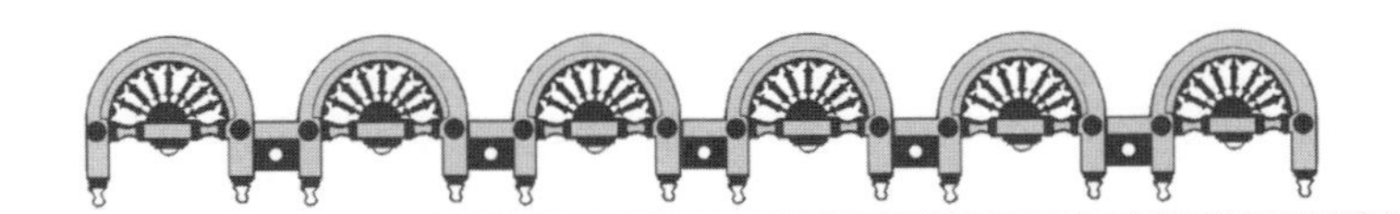

World's Best Cookie

- 1 cup butter, unsalted
- 1 cup sugar
- 1 cup brown sugar, firmly packed
- 1 cups salad oil
- 1 t vanilla
- 1 egg
- 1 cup oats
- 1 cup crushed corn flakes
- ½ cup shredded coconut
- ½ cup chopped walnuts or pecans
- 3½ cups four
- 1 t baking soda
- 1 t salt
- extra sugar for topping

Mix together flour, baking soda and salt. Cream butter and sugars and salad oil add vanilla and egg and beat well. Add flour mixture, then add oats, corn flakes, coconut and nuts, beat until combined. Drop by teaspoon full on baking sheet and flatten with a fork that has been dipped in water. Bake for 10-12 minutes at 325°. After removing from baking sheet, sprinkle each cookie with sugar while still warm.

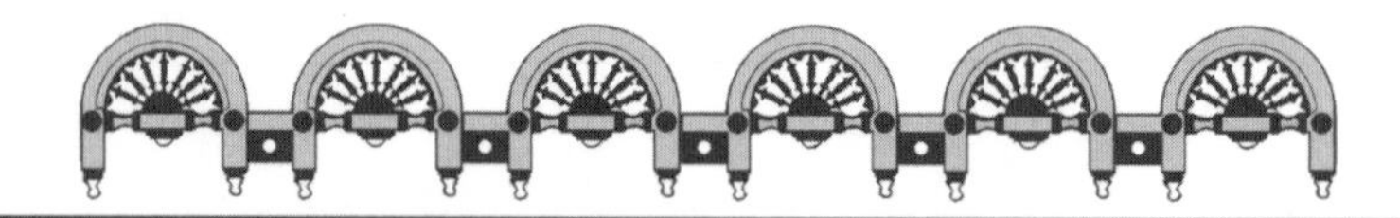

Finger Cookies

Combine flour and salt. Cream butter and Crisco, add vanilla then flour and beat until combined. Shape dough into small long rolls and place on a greased cookie sheet, then flatten each roll with your finger. Brush with egg that has been mixed with a few drops of milk and sprinkle some nuts on top. Bake at 375°until golden. Remove from oven and slice the cookies on a diagonal about 1" thick. Remove to rack to cool. Store in an airtight container.

¾ cup butter, softened
¾ cup Crisco
1 t vanilla
3 cups flour
½ t salt
1 egg, beaten (for a glaze)
chopped walnuts
milk

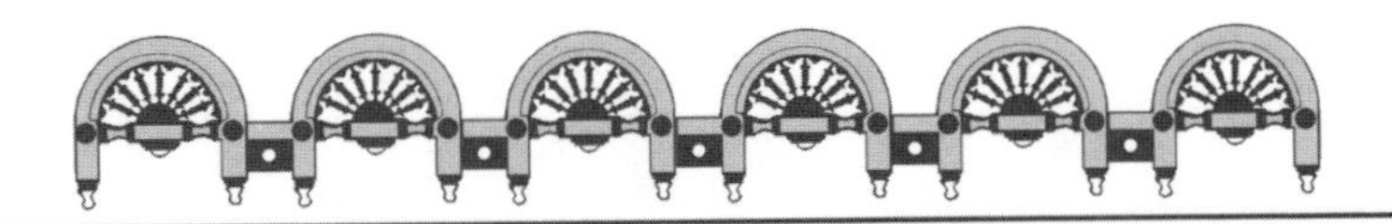

Danish Overnight Cookies

- 1 cup butter, softened
- 2 cups sugar
- 2 eggs, slightly beaten
- 1 cup walnuts
- 3 ½ cups flour
- 1 t baking powder
- ¼ t baking soda
- 2 t vanilla

Mix dry ingredients. Cream butter and sugar until light and fluffy. Add beaten eggs and vanilla, then add flour mixture and blend well. Mix in nuts. Divide into 4 round balls. Roll each ball out into a long roll and wrap in waxed paper. Chill in refrigerator overnight. Slice and bake on lightly greased baking sheets for 10-12 minutes at 375°. Store in airtight container.

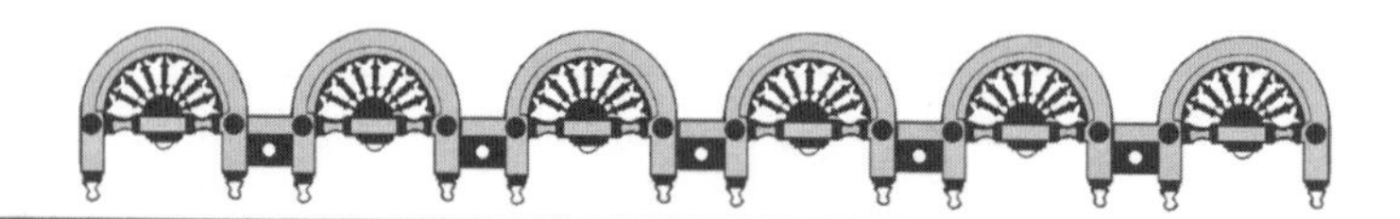

Great Grandma's Raisin Filled Cookies

½ cup butter
½ cup lard
2 cups brown sugar
1 cup white sugar
2 eggs
1 t vanilla
1 cup sour cream
4½ cups flour
3 scant t baking soda

Raisin Filling
½ box of raisins, ground or put through a food processor
1½ T flour
1 cup sugar
1 cup boiling water

Combine baking soda with flour. Cream lard, butter and sugars until light and fluffy. Add eggs and vanilla, then sour cream. Beat well to combine. Add flour gradually. Cover dough and chill for several hours or overnight. Roll dough out to 1/8" thickness on a well-floured surface. Cut out cookies with a 2" cookie cutter. Place a cookie on a lightly greased baking sheet. Put 1 teaspoon of filling in the center. Place another cookie on top and press the edges together lightly to seal. Repeat with remaining cookies. Bake for 12 minutes in a 350°oven. Remove to wire rack to cool.

Raisin Filling

Combine all ingredients and cook until thick. Cool completely and refrigerate for several hours or overnight covered.

Makes 8 dozen.

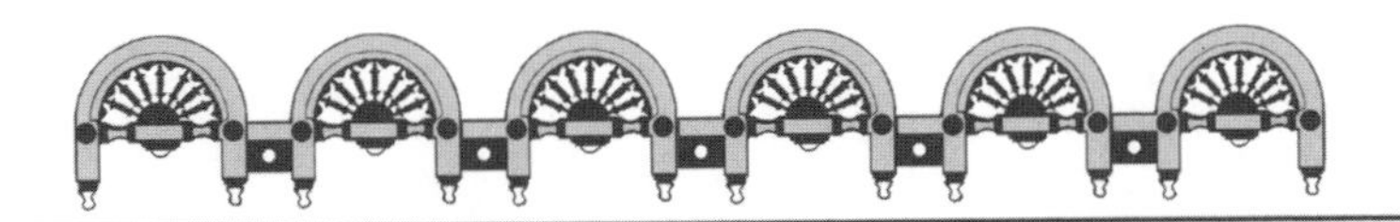

Sweet Rich Sugar Cookie

1 cup butter, unsalted
1 cup vegetable oil
1½ cups granulated sugar
1 cup confectioner's sugar
2 eggs, large
4¼ cups flour
1 t baking soda
1 t cream of tartar
½ t salt

In a large mixing bowl cream butter, oil, 1 cup of granulated sugar and confectioner's sugar until creamy. Add eggs, 1 at a time beating well after each addition.

Mix together flour, soda, salt and cream of tartar. Thoroughly blend dry ingredients into butter mixture. Place remaining ½ cup sugar into a small bowl. Shape dough into 1" balls and drop into bowl of sugar and coat each one completely. Place balls 3 inches apart on an ungreased cookie sheet. Dip the bottom of a glass in sugar and flatten each cookie to about ¼" thickness. Bake at 375° for about 10 to 12 minutes or until edges are lightly browned. Cool completely on wire rack. Store in airtight container.

Makes 8 dozen.

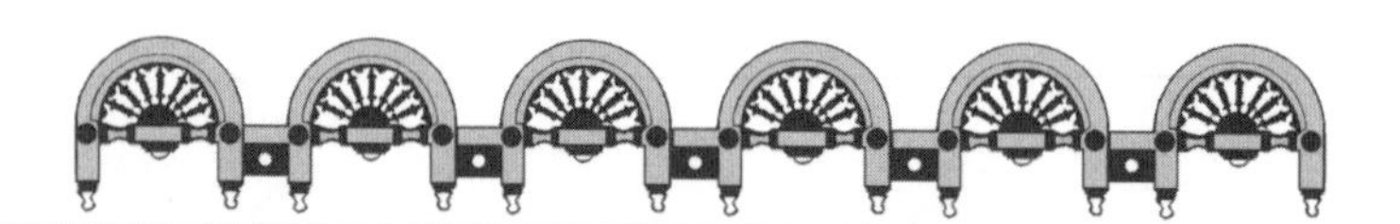

Kipfel (German Butterhorn)

A traditional German cookie served with afternoon tea.

Combine water and sugar then stir in yeast and set side for 10 minutes. Place flour in bowl, cut in butter, then add yeast mixture, egg yolks and sour cream. Mix well, form into ball and knead for 5 minutes. Divide into 3 parts and wrap and chill for 1 hour. Sprinkle work surface with confectioner's sugar, roll dough out into circle and cut in the 12 wedges.

Filling

Make filling by combing nuts, sugar and vanilla. Beat egg whites with cream of tartar until stiff, then fold into nut mixture. Fill wide end of dough with 1 teaspoon filling and spread toward narrow end. Roll up from wide end to narrow end. Repeat with remaining dough. Bake in 350° on lightly greased sheet for 15 minutes.

2 T warm water
¼ t sugar
1 T yeast
2 cups flour
½ cup butter
2 egg yolks
½ cup sour cream
confectioner's sugar

Filling
1 cup finely chopped walnuts
½ cup sugar
1 t vanilla
2 egg whites
pinch of cream of tarter

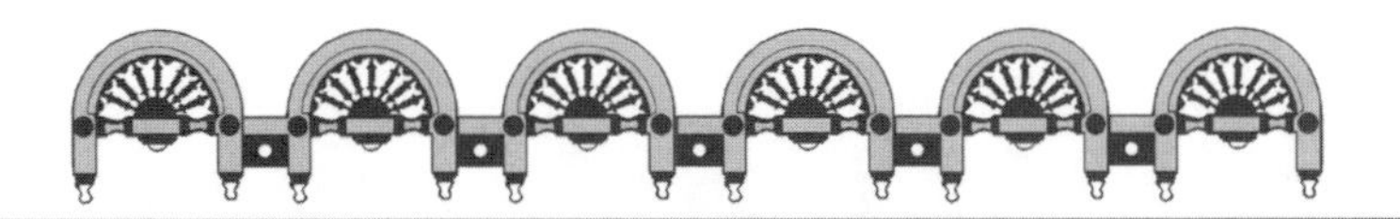

Date Pinwheel Overnight Cookies

Filling
½ lb. dates, finely chopped
⅓ cup water
¼ cup sugar
¼ cup finely chopped walnuts

Cookie
½ cup butter, softened
½ cup white sugar
½ cup brown sugar
1 egg, well beaten
2 cups flour
½ t baking soda
¼ t salt

Filling

Mix dates, water and sugar together and boil for 5 minutes. Remove from heat and add walnuts. Cool

Cookie

Cream butter and sugars, add egg and blend. Add flour that has been mixed with soda and salt and blend until all the flour is incorporated. Divide dough in half. Roll dough out on floured surface to ¼" thickness. Spread cooled date mixture on dough. Gently roll up dough lengthwise like a jelly roll. Wrap in waxed paper. Repeat with second section of dough. Chill in refrigerator overnight.

Slice and bake on lightly greased sheet for 12 minutes or until lightly browned. 375° oven.

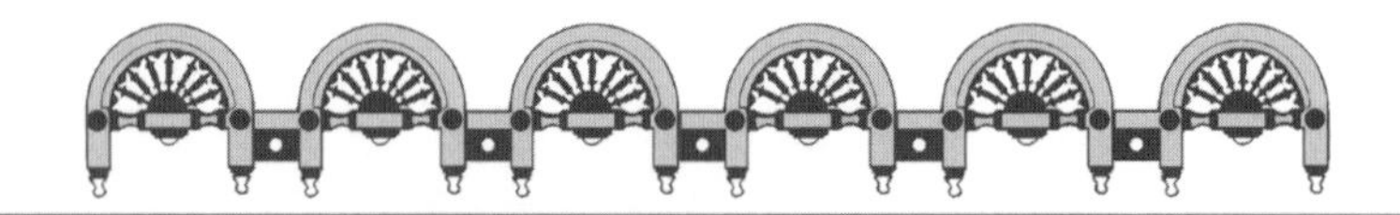

Danish Sprutter (Spritz Cookie)

Cream butter and sugar until light and fluffy, about 3 minutes. Add egg and beat well., then flour and vanilla. Put through a cookie press using your favorite shapes. Bake on ungreased cookie sheet in 375°oven until golden, about 12 minutes.

1½ cups butter, softened
1 cup sugar
1 egg
1 t vanilla
3 cups flour

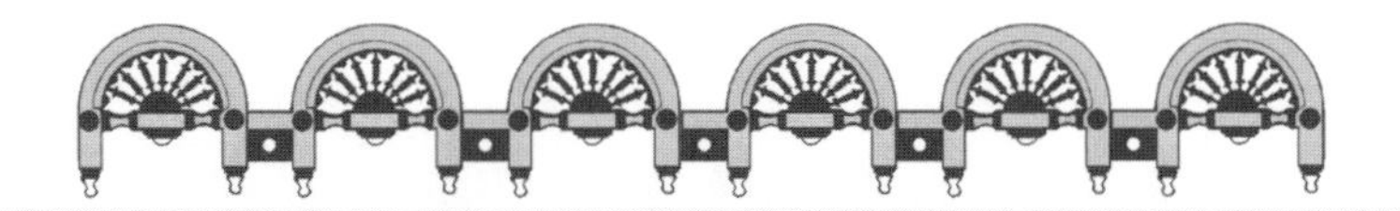

White Biscotti

¾ cup butter, softened
1 cup sugar
3 eggs
3 cups flour
½ t salt
1 t baking powder
1 cup chopped almonds
1 ½ T anise seed
1 t anise flavoring
confectioner's sugar

Preheat oven to 325°.

Cream butter and sugar until light and fluffy, add eggs one at a time.

Mix flour, salt and baking powder well, then add chopped almonds, anise seed and anise flavoring.

Turn out on floured board and kneed several times until smooth.

Divide dough into 4 equal parts and roll each one out into a log shape. Place on non- greased cookie sheet. Flatten log slightly and bake in 325° oven for 20 minutes.

Take out of oven and slice diagonally into ½" to ¾" slices. Separate apart, place cut side down on baking sheet and return to oven and bake for an additional 7-10 minutes. When cool, dip each cookie into confectioner's sugar to coat.

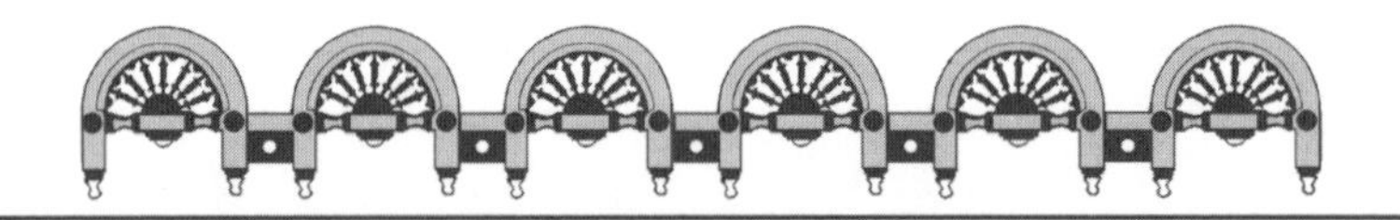

Cream Wafers with Butter Filling

Wafers
1 cup butter, softened
2 cups flour
1/3 cup heavy cream

Filling
1/4 cup butter, softened
3/4 cup sifted confectioner's sugar
1 egg yolk
1 t vanilla

Wafers

Mix thoroughly. Spread filling on bottom side of cookie and place another cookie on top. Filling may be tinted with food coloring.

Filling

Slowly mix cream into softened butter. Scrape down sides of bowl and add flour and mix well. Wrap and chill for 1 hour. Roll out dough on floured surface to 1/8" thick. Cut into rounds with a 1½" cookie cutter. Transfer to a sheet of waxed paper that has been heavily sprinkled with granulated sugar, turning to coat both sides. Place on an ungreased baking sheet. Prick in 4 places with a fork and bake at 375° for 7-9 minutes, or until slightly puffy. Cool completely on rack.

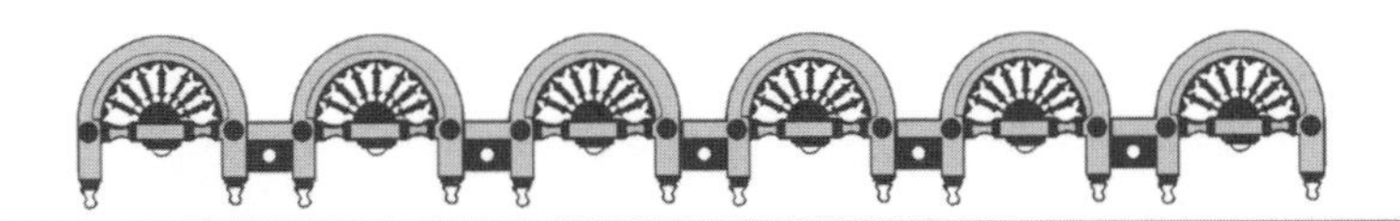

Chocolate Lovers Biscotti

- 3 cups all purpose flour
- ¾ cup sugar
- ½ cup brown sugar, packed
- 1 t baking powder
- ¾ t salt
- 3 oz. unsweetened baking chocolate, melted & cooled
- 3 eggs, large
- ⅓ cup olive oil
- 2 T each orange juice & rum
- 1 T grated orange peel
- 1 t vanilla
- 1 cup semi-sweet chocolate chips
- 1 cup chopped almonds
- 12-14 oz. white chocolate for dipping

In a large bowl combine flour, sugars, baking powder and salt. Add cooled, melted unsweetened chocolate, eggs, oil, juice, rum, orange peel and vanilla. Stir to combine. Add chocolate chips and almonds; mix until dough is well blended.

Roll dough in ball and cut into four equal portions, shaping each section into a log about 2" wide by 12-14" long. Place two logs on each of two lightly greased baking sheets, and flatten logs gently. Bake at 350° for 20 minutes. Remove from oven and cool for 45-60 seconds. Using a serrated knife cut diagonally into ½ inch-wide slices. Place slices cut side down on baking sheets and return to oven; bake for an additional 15 minutes of until crisp. Cool on wire racks.

Meanwhile, melt white chocolate in a double boiler over medium heat, stirring until smooth (vegetable oil may be added to the chocolate a teaspoon at a time if chocolate it too thick for dipping). Dip each cookie about 1" into the melted chocolate to coat. Lay on wire rack until cool and set. Store in airtight container.

Yield: 6 dozen cookies.

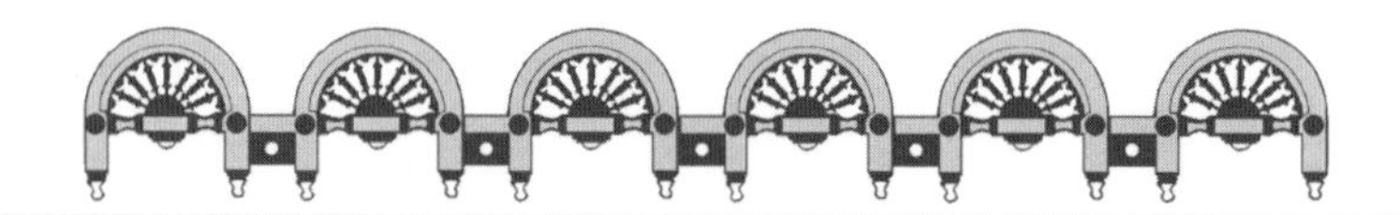

Cheesecake Bars

Mix condensed milk and lemon juice and rind and let stand.

Mix together flour, soda, salt and oatmeal.

Mix butter and sugar. Cream well. Add the rest of the dry ingredients. Place ½ of the crumb mixture in a large jelly roll pan (12x16") and press firmly in place. Spread the condensed milk mixture over the top. Then cover with the rest of the crumb mixture.

Bake at 325° for 25-30 minutes.

2 cans condensed milk
1 cup lemon juice
2 T lemon rind
⅓ cup softened butter
2 cups brown sugar
3½ cups flour
1 t soda
2 t salt
3 cups oatmeal

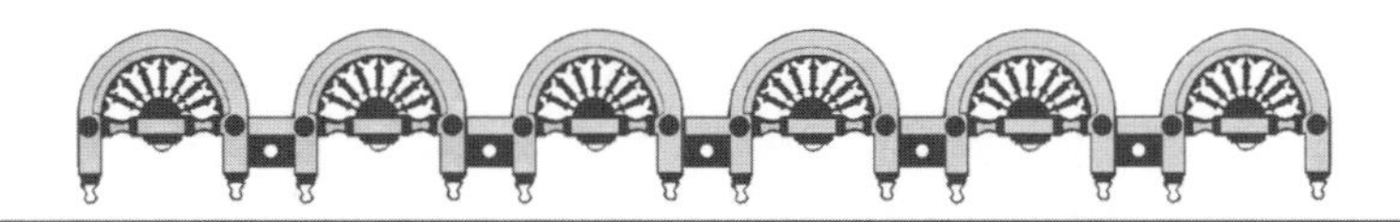

Gingerbread Mansion's Lemon Bars

Crust
2½ cups unbleached flour
⅔ cup confectioner's sugar
1 cup butter, chilled and cut into small pieces
¼ cup margarine, chilled and cut into small pieces

Filling
5 eggs
2½ cup granulated sugar
6 T lemon juice
½ cup all-purpose flour
¾ t baking soda

Crust

In large mixing bowl combine flour, sugar, butter and margarine. Beat at low speed for one minute, then at medium speed until crumbly.

Press dough into ungreased 12x16" jelly roll pan.

Bake at 350° for 15-20 minutes or until crust is firm, but not brown.

Filling

In small mixing bowl combine eggs, sugar and lemon juice. Add flour mixed with baking soda. Beat at low speed just until blended. Pour over hot baked crust (pan will be very full). Bake for an additional 25 minutes or until set slightly browned. Cool on wire rack. Cut into squares or diamond and dust with powdered sugar.

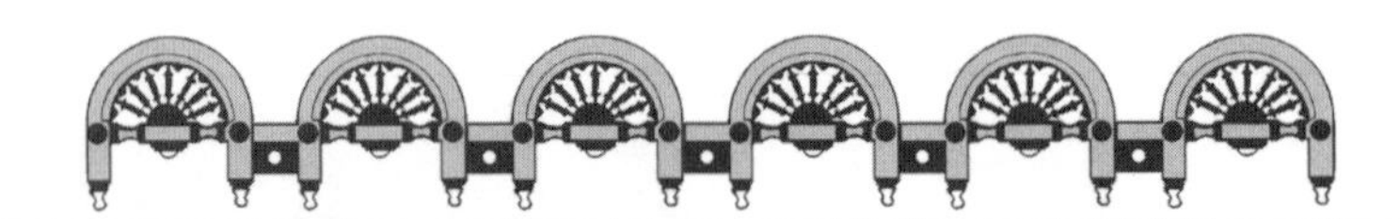

Southern Pecan Bars

Bottom Layer

Mix flour and sugar together. Cut in butter. Add pecans and mix well. Pack mixture into 12x16" jelly roll pan. Bake for 10 minutes at 350°.

Topping

While crust is baking, beat eggs until foamy. Add corn syrup, sugar, flour, salt and vanilla, mixing well. Pour topping on baked crust and sprinkle with pecans. Bake for 20-30 minutes at 350°. Cool. Cut into squares.

Bottom Layer
- 2 cups flour
- 2/3 cup brown sugar, packed
- ½ cup butter
- ½ cup chopped pecans

Topping
- 4 eggs
- 1½ cup dark corn syrup
- ½ cup brown sugar
- 4 T flour
- 1 t salt
- 2 t vanilla
- 1½ cups chopped pecans

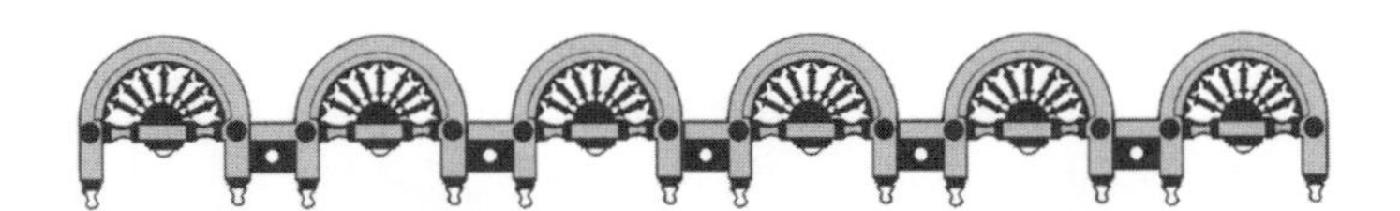

Chocolate Streusel Bars

- 1¾ cups unsifted all-purpose flour
- 1½ cups confectioner's sugar
- ½ cup unsweetened cocoa powder
- 1 cup cold butter (2 sticks)
- 1 8 oz. package cream cheese, softened
- 1 14 oz. can sweetened condensed milk
- 1 egg
- 2 t vanilla extract
- ½ cup chopped walnuts

In large bowl, combine flour, sugar, and cocoa. Cut in butter with pastry blender until crumbly, (mixture will be dry). Reserve 2 cups crumb mixture. Press remaining crumb mixture onto bottom of a 13x9" baking pan. Bake for 15 minutes.

In a large bowl beat cream cheese until fluffy. Gradually beat in condensed milk until smooth. Add egg and vanilla. Mix well. Pour over prepared crust. Combine nuts and reserved crumb mixture. Sprinkle evenly over the top of the cheese mixture.

Bake for 20 minutes at 350° or until bubbly and set.

Cool and chill. Cut into bars. Store in refrigerator.

Yields 24

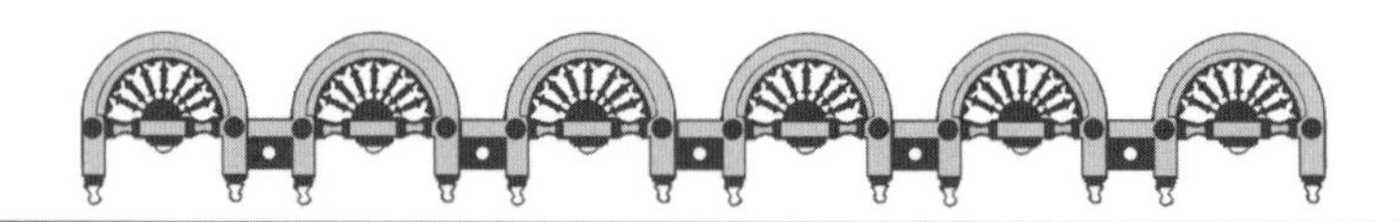

Maylane's Brandied Fruit Bars

2 cups confectioner's sugar
½ cup butter softened
¼ cup brandy
2 eggs
2 cups flour
1 t baking powder
1 t salt
2 cups mixed candied cake fruits
1 cup chopped walnuts

Combine flour, baking powder and salt. Cream butter and sugar. Add Brandy and eggs and beat well. Slowly add flour mixture and beat until combined. Stir in candied fruit and nuts. Press into a greased jelly roll pan 10x15" bake for 15-20 minutes at 375°, cool in pan. When cool, spread glaze on top and when glaze has set, cut into squares and store in an airtight container.

Glaze

1 cup confectioner's sugar
1 T butter, softened
1½ T Brandy

Combine until creamy.

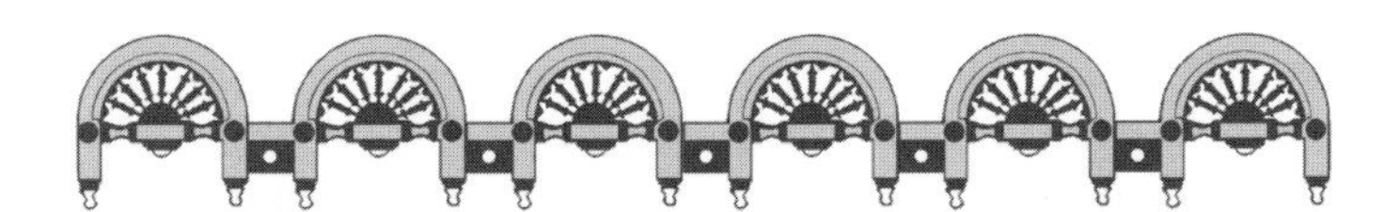

Melt in your Mouth Butter Bars

Butter Cake Layer
1½ cups flour
1½ t baking powder
½ t salt
¾ cup sugar
1½ cubes unsalted butter, softened
2 eggs, large and room temperature
1¼ t vanilla
½ cup whole milk

Topping
1 8 oz. package cream cheese, softened
2 eggs, large
4 cups confectioner's sugar, sifted, divided
¼ t almond extract
2 t vanilla extract
½ cup pecans lightly toasted then finely chopped
2 oz. white chocolate, melted

Butter Cake Layer

Generously butter an 12x16" jelly roll pan, set aside. Sift flour, baking powder and salt together. In a large bowl of an electric mixer, using a whisk attachment, cream the butter and sugar until light and fluffy, about 3 minutes. Add the eggs one at a time and beat thoroughly. Add the vanilla. Spoon in the flour mixture alternately with the milk, blending until the batter is smooth, being careful not to over mix. Pour the batter into the prepared pan and spread evenly. Meanwhile, prepare topping.

Topping

In a large bowl of an electric mixer, fitted with the paddle attachment, beat the cream cheese, eggs, 3 cups of the confectioner's sugar and the almond and vanilla extracts at low speed until smooth, increase the speed to high and beat for 5 minutes. Reduce speed to low and add remaining cup of sugar. Beat mixture 5 minutes more at high speed. Pour the mixture over the butter cake layer and bake for 35-40 minutes at 325° or until top is lightly browned. Cool completely in pan, on a rack for 30 minutes. Drizzle the melted chocolate decoratively over the top and sprinkle with the nuts. Chill the bars in the refrigerator until the chocolate is set. Slice into bars with a knife periodically running it under hot water. Store in airtight container.

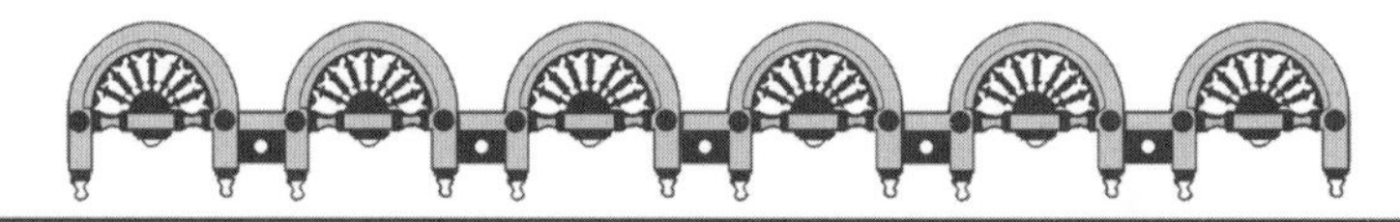

Swedish Coconut Bars

Three individual layers make these bars rich and delicious.

First Layer

Combine flour, sugar and cornstarch in a mixer bowl, cut butter into small pieces and add to flour mixture, beat on medium speed until the mixture holds together. Press into an 11x15" jelly roll pan. Bake in 300° oven for 20 minutes or until just beginning to get golden.

Second Layer

Mix all ingredients until well blended and spread on baked first layer. Bake 15-20 minutes at 325° or until mixture is set. Cool completely.

Third Layer

Cream butter and cream cheese until light and fluffy. Gradually add confectioner's sugar and mix well. Spread over the top of cooled coconut bars. Let stand until icing sets up, then cut into bars and store covered in the refrigerator. Freezes well.

First Layer
- 1 cup unsalted butter
- 2 cups flour
- ½ cup sugar
- ½ cup cornstarch

Second Layer
- 1 8oz. package shredded coconut
- 4 eggs beaten
- 2¼ cups brown sugar, packed
- 2 t vanilla
- 4 T flour
- ½ t baking powder
- 2 cups walnuts, chopped

Third Layer
- 1 8 oz. package cream cheese, softened
- ¼ cup unsalted butter, softened
- 1 lb. confectioner's sugar

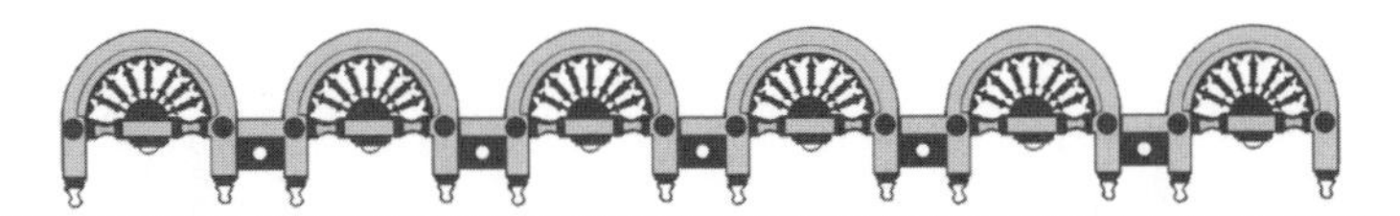

Rum Raisin Squares

- 3 T butter, softened
- 2/3 cup firmly packed brown sugar
- 1 egg
- 2 T molasses
- 4 t light rum
- ½ t vanilla
- ¾ cup unbleached flour
- ½ t baking powder
- ¼ t salt
- ¼ t cinnamon
- ¼ t nutmeg
- ½ cup raisins, coarsely chopped
- ½ cup chocolate chips
- fine, dry breadcrumbs
- ¼ cup confectioner's sugar

Cream butter and brown sugar until fluffy. Add the egg, molasses. 3 tablespoons of rum and vanilla, beat until blended. Sift the flour, baking powder, salt, cinnamon and nutmeg, add to the batter and beat until well mixed. Stir in the raisins and chocolate chips.

Grease an 8" square baking dish with butter and dust with breadcrumbs. Spread the batter evenly into the pan and bake at 350° for 20-25 minutes, until top is firm and the cake begins to pull away from the sides of the pan. Mix the confectioner's sugar with the remaining 1 teaspoon rum and dribble over the warm cake.

Cool the cake in the pan and cut into 24 bars. Store in airtight container. Leftovers may be frozen.

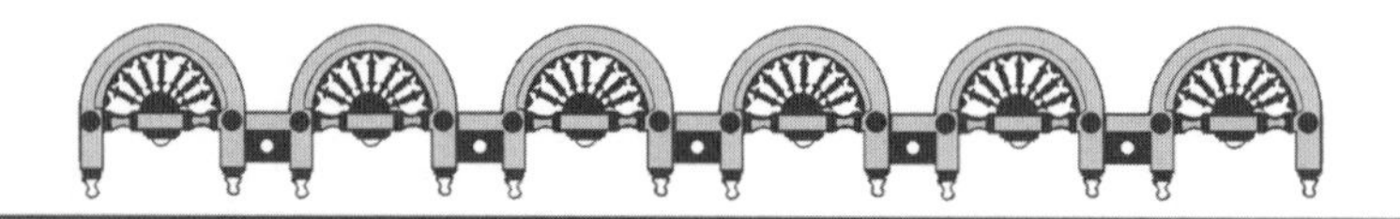

Marnie's Carmel Pecan Squares

Crust
3 cups flour
1 ½ cups butter, cut into small pieces
½ cup sugar
1½ cups milk chocolate chips

Filling
2⅔ cups sugar
⅔ cup light corn syrup
2 cups butter (1 lb.)
2 cups whipping cream
5 cups chopped pecans
4 oz. white chocolate chips, melted

Crust

To prepare crust, combine flour, butter and sugar in medium bowl. Mix with pastry blender or a fork until well blended. Press into a lightly greased 12x15" pan. Bake until lightly browned, about 15-20minutes at 350°. Remove from oven and sprinkle with the milk chocolate chips, let stand 2 minutes then spread chocolate over crust. Set aside.

Filling

To prepare filling, place sugar in a heavy saucepan, cook and stir over low heat until the sugar melts and is caramel colored, about 20 minutes. This is a slow process as there is no liquid mixed with the sugar. Slowly stir in the corn syrup, butter and cream. Cook over medium heat until mixture reaches 240° on a candy thermometer. Remove from heat and stir in pecans. Immediately pour over the crust, smoothing to make an even layer. Refrigerate. Melt the white chocolate and drizzle over the cooled bars. Cut into small squares.

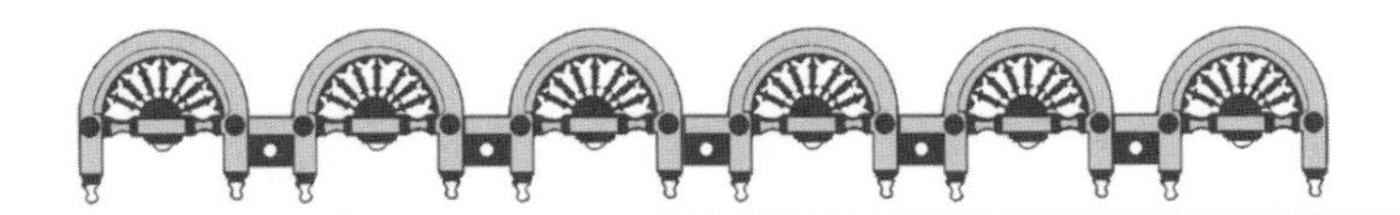

May's Sliced Almond Bars

Pastry
½ cup butter
1¼ cups flour
¼ cup sugar
1 egg yolk beaten
½ t almond extract

Filling
3 T butter
2 T milk
½ cup sugar
1 T honey
1 cup sliced almonds

Pastry

In large bowl cut butter into flour and sugar suing a pastry blender until crumbly. Stir in egg yolk and almond extract. With hands, work into a ball. Wrap and chill for 1 hour.

Preheat oven to 325°, press dough evenly into an 8x11" baking dish. Bake until golden, about 30 minutes

Filling

In saucepan heat butter and milk. Add sugar, honey and almonds and stir well. Spread filling over cooked pastry and return to oven and bake for an additional 20-30 minutes until golden and bubbly. Cool on rack for 10 minutes. Cut into diamonds or 1½" squares.

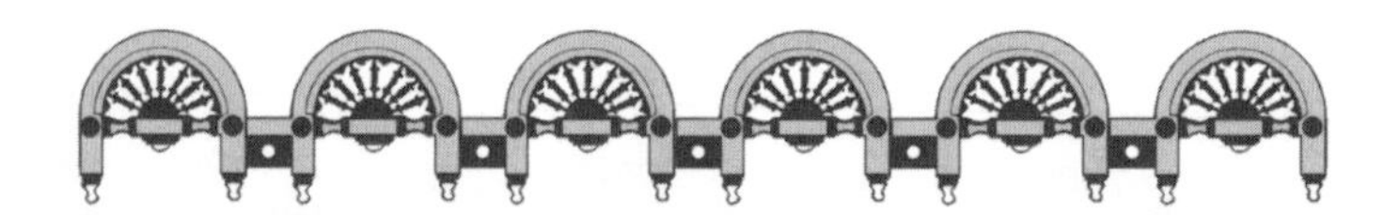

Frosted Fudge Squares

Preheat oven to 375°. In small saucepan, melt chocolate and butter. Set aside to cool. In bowl of electric mixer, beat eggs, sugar, vanilla and salt. Beat 8 minutes until mixture is light and expanded in volume. Beat in chocolate mixture, then by hand stir in flour and nuts. Pour batter into a well-greased 9x13" pan. Bake 30-35 minutes or until done. Do not over bake!

8 oz. unsweetened chocolate
1 cup butter
5 eggs
3 cups sugar
2 t vanilla
½ t salt
1½ cups all purpose flour
¾ cup chopped walnuts

Frosting

Melt chocolate in top of double boiler. As soon as chocolate is smooth and melted, remove from heat and stir in sour cream and vanilla. It will thicken as it cools. Spread on cooled fudge bars. Sprinkle top with nuts and cut into squares.

Frosting
12 oz. semi-sweet chocolate chips
1 cup sour cream
1 t vanilla

Yields 40 bars.

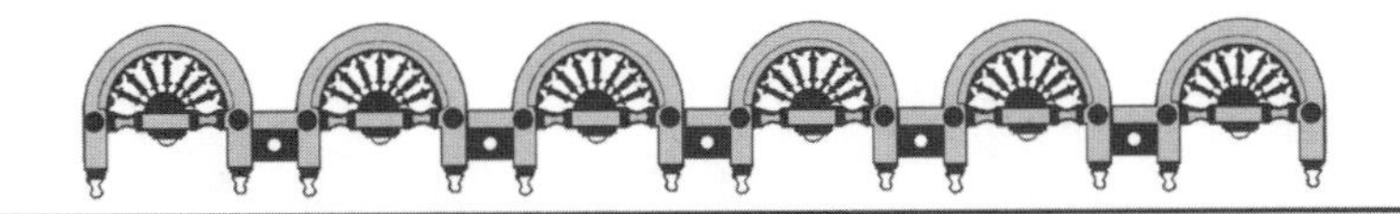

Rich Short Pastry

1 $2/3$ cup all-purpose flour
$1/8$ t salt
5-6 T confectioner's sugar or granulated sugar
$3/4$ cup unsalted butter, chilled and diced into small pieces
1 extra large egg yolk
Ice water as needed to bind dough together

A sweet, rich pastry that is excellent for tarts and mini-tarts.

Combine flour, salt and sugar. Cut in butter until coarse meal is formed. Add egg yolk and enough water to bind dough together. Roll in ball and wrap and chill for 30 minutes before rolling out.

Will make 3 dozen mini-tartlet shells.

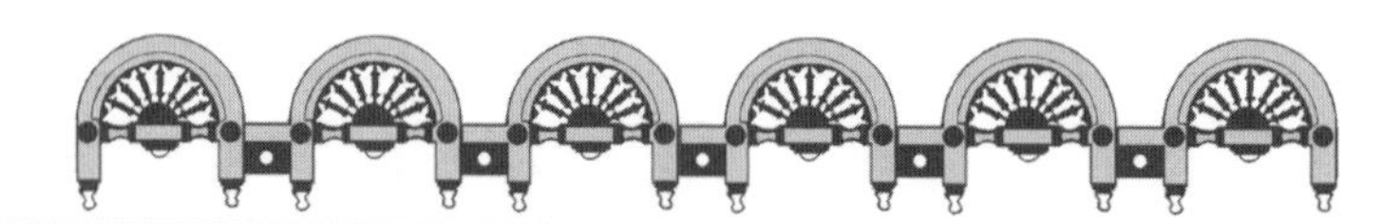

Basic Pastry for Individual Tart Shells

Blend flour and salt. Cut in butter and shortening. Sprinkle with 3 tablespoons ice water and mix to incorporate. Add more water if needed. Chill 1 hour before rolling out and cutting in desired shapes.

1 ¾ cups flour
½ t salt
½ cup + 1 T cold unsalted butter (cut into bits)
3 T cold vegetable shortening
3-5 T ice water

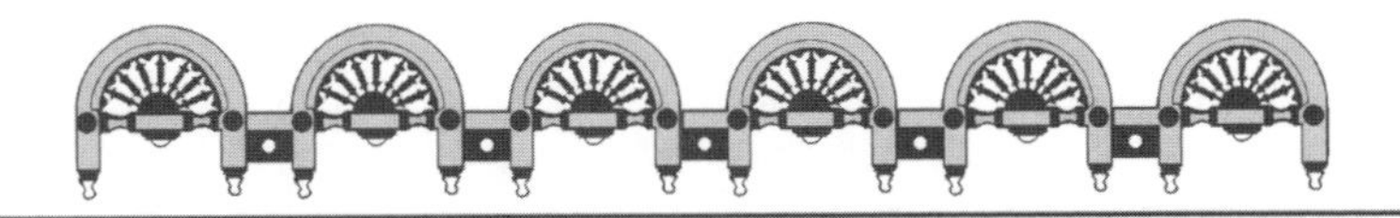

Tart Pastry #1

- 1 cup unsalted butter, softened
- 1/3 cup sugar
- 1 t vanilla
- 1 egg
- 2½ cups flour

This tart pastry is more like a cookie dough rather than a pie crust and is very good.

Cream softened butter with sugar. Add vanilla and then beat in egg. Blend in flour. Wrap and chill for 4 hours to overnight. When ready to use, cut off a third of the dough at a time, keeping the remainder in the refrigerator until ready to use. Roll out to 1/8" thickness and cut out with appropriate size cookie cutter. Press into mini muffin tins or tart tins.

Bake in 350° oven for 12-15 minutes. When cool, fill with your choice of tart fillings.

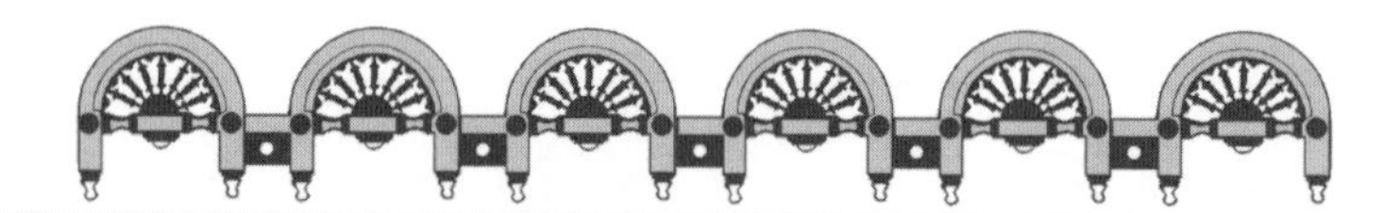

Tart Pastry #2

Blend flour, sugar and salt. Cut in butter and vegetable shortening until mix forms a coarse meal. Add enough ice water to bind mixture. Wrap and chill for 1 hour.

- 2½ cups flour
- 2 T sugar
- ½ t salt
- 1½ cubes cold unsalted butter, cut into small pieces
- 4 T cold vegetable shortening
- 4 T or more ice water

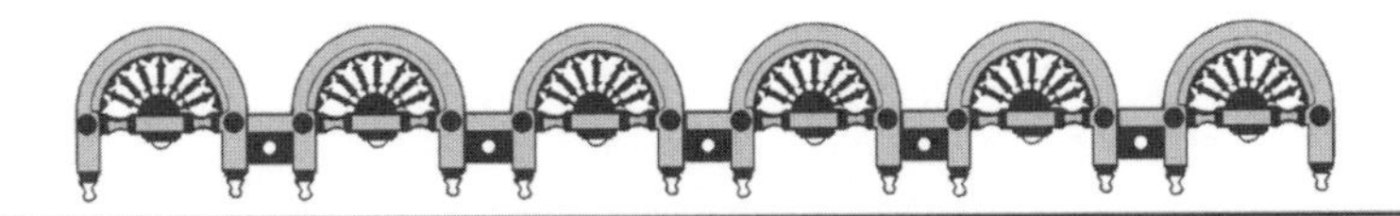

Lemon Curd Tartlets

3 eggs
5 T butter, melted
1 cup sugar
juice and grated rind of two lemons

Beat eggs into melted butter, then stir in sugar. Beat until thoroughly combined. Add lemon juice and rind gradually.

Cook over a double-boiler until thickened, stirring constantly. Cool completely and chill.

Fill individual baked tart shells and top each with a dollop of whipped cream and a sprinkle of lemon zest just before serving.

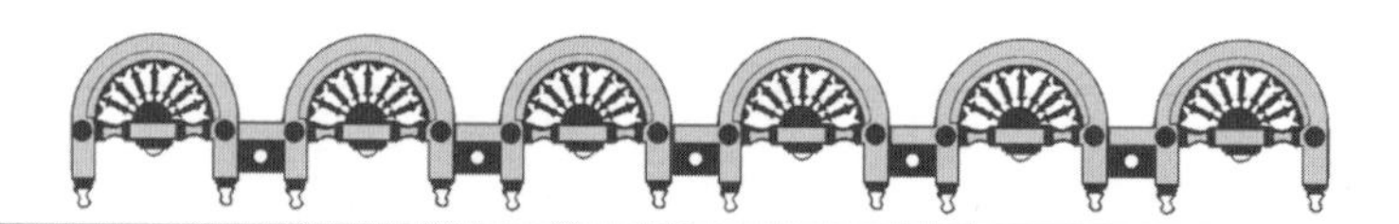

Mincemeat Tarts

These tarts are special when prepared with homemade mincemeat. See recipe for Homemade Mincemeat.

½ cup butter, softened
3 oz. cream cheese, softened
1 cup flour

In a small mixer bowl, beat together butter and cream cheese. Stir in flour. Roll into a ball and wrap and chill for 1 hour. Shape dough into 1 inch balls. Press onto the bottom and up the sides of ungreased mini-muffin tins.

Filling

1 ¼ cup homemade or purchased mincemeat
½ cup chopped walnuts
1 T finely shredded orange peel
2 T finely shredded lemon peel

In mixing bowl, stir together mincemeat, walnuts, orange peel and lemon peel. Place one rounded teaspoon of filling in each cup. Bake in 350° oven for 25-30 minutes or until done. Cool slightly in pan then remove and cool on a wire rack.

Makes 24.

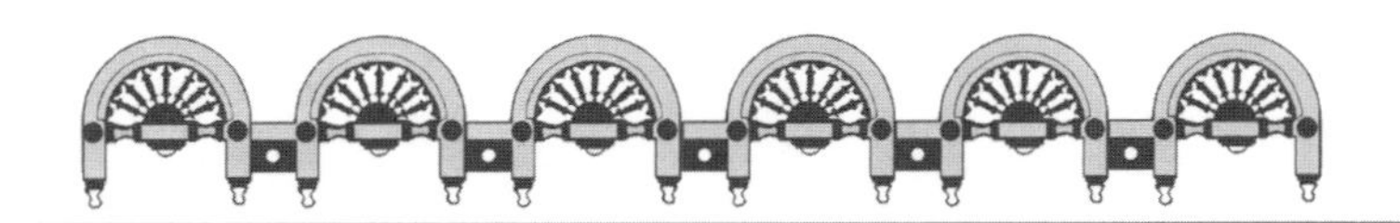

Chocolate Coffee Cream Tart Filling

1 cup whipping cream
3 T sugar
½ t instant coffee powder
1 oz. semi-sweet chocolate
2 dozen baked pastry tart shells, cooled

Combine cream, sugar and coffee in heavy saucepan. Place over low heat and stir until sugar and coffee are dissolved. Slowly bring to a boil, stirring frequently to avoid burning and cook until mixture is reduced to ¾ cup. Remove from heat, add chocolate and stir until completely melted.

Let cool for 10 minutes before pouring into tart shells. When cool, decorate with chocolate sprinkles, shaved chocolate or a candy coffee bean.

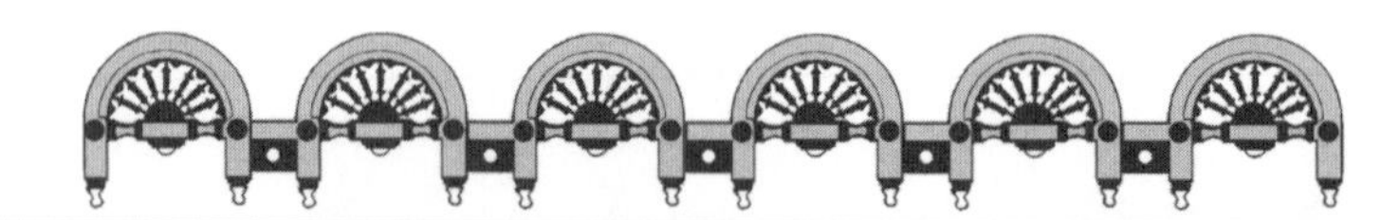

Frangipane Tart Filling

- 4 oz. almond paste, room temperature, broken into pieces
- 1/3 cup sugar
- 2 T butter, softened
- 2 eggs, slightly beaten
- 1 t vanilla
- 1 t dark rum
- 1 t finely grated lemon zest
- 2 dozen unbaked tart shells

Using a mixer or food processor, combine almond paste and sugar until thoroughly combined. Beat in butter. Slowly add eggs and flavorings until completely incorporated and mixture is smooth.

Spoon 1 teaspoon filling into each unbaked tart shell, sprinkle each with a few sliced almonds and bake for 15 minutes at 350°. When cool, remove from tins and brush each tart with some warmed apricot jam.

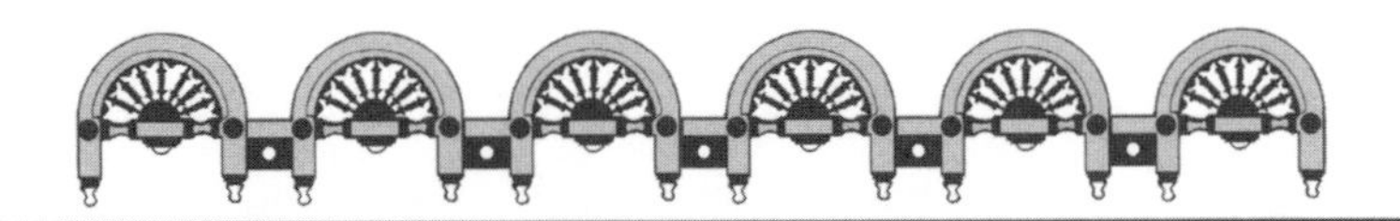

Buttermilk Tart

- 1 recipe tart pastry
- 1 10″ tart pan with removable bottom
- 6 T unsalted butter, softened
- 1 cup sugar
- 2 eggs separated at room temperature
- 3 T flour
- 1 T fresh lemon juice
- ½ t freshly grated nutmeg
- ¼ t salt
- 1 cup buttermilk, room temperature
- fresh raspberries
- confectioner's sugar

In bowl of electric mixer, combine the butter and sugar until the sugar is completely incorporated, about 3 minutes. Add the egg yolks and mix well to combine. Add the flour, lemon juice, nutmeg and salt. Slowly add in the buttermilk.

In another bowl, whip the egg whites until they form soft peaks. Pour a little of the buttermilk mixture into the egg whites and fold gently to combine. Gently fold egg white mixture into the remaining buttermilk mixture until just combined. Pour the mixture into the baked pie shell. Bake in a 350° oven until lightly browned and barely moves when the pie is jiggled, about 45 minutes. Cool on rack.

Serve at room temperature with fresh raspberries and confectioner's sugar sprinkled on top.

Tart pastry baking directions

Heat oven to 400°. On a lightly floured surface roll out pastry dough into a 14" round, about 1/8" thick. Place the dough into a 10-inch removable bottom tart pan with flutted sides. Trim off excess and press dough to conform with edges on pan. Line the dough with a piece of foil or parchment paper and weight it with dried beans or pie weights.

Bake for 12 minutes. Remove the weights and the foil and bake until crust is golden, about 5-7 minutes.

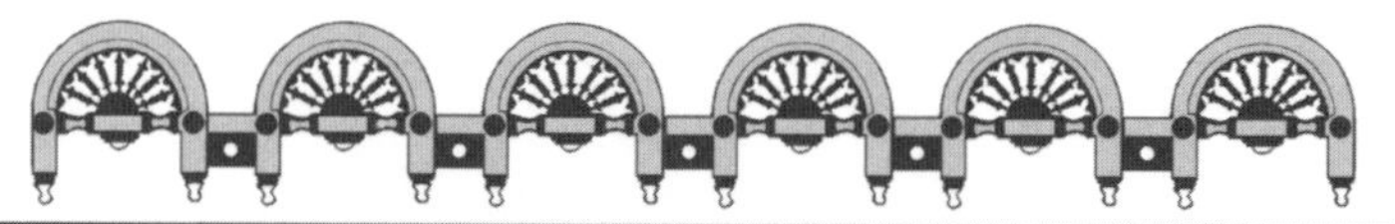

Rum Custard for Fruit Tarts

- ¼ cup sugar
- 3 T flour
- 1 envelope gelatin
- 2 large eggs
- 1 large egg yolk
- 1½ cups whole milk
- 3 T light rum or ½ t rum extract
- ½ cup heavy cream

In a medium saucepan, combine sugar, flour and gelatin. In small bowl beat eggs, yolk and milk. Stir liquid into sugar mixture. Cook over medium-low heat, stirring constantly until mixture thickens and begins to boil. Remove from heat. Cover and chill until mixture begins to mound slightly (about one hour). Stir in rum. Beat cream to soft peaks. Fold into custard.

Spoon into prepared baked shells and top with fresh berries and a wedge of kiwi.

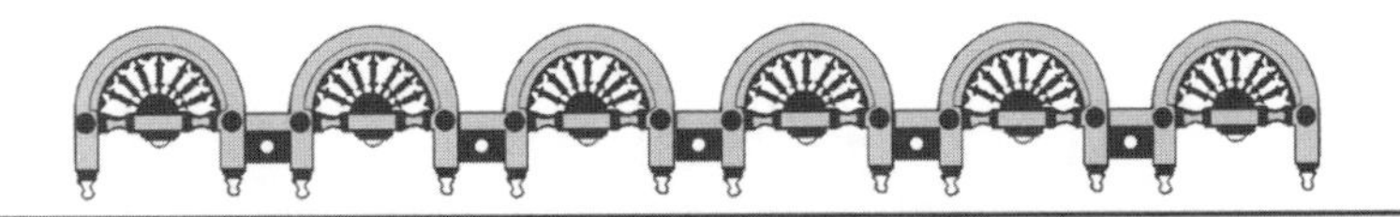

Triple-Chocolate Pot de Crème

- 3 oz. fine quality semi-sweet chocolate, chopped
- 3 oz. unsweetened chocolate chopped
- ¼ cup unsalted butter, cut into bits
- 3 cups whole milk
- 1 2″ piece of vanilla bean, split lengthwise
- 2 large eggs
- 4 large egg yolks
- 1 cup sugar
- 2 t cornstarch
- 1 cup heavy cream
- ½ cup unsweetened cocoa powder

In a metal bowl set over a pan of barely simmering water, melt the chocolates with the butter, stirring until mixture is smooth. Let the mixture cool. In a saucepan, bring the milk to a simmer with the vanilla bean and scrape the vanilla bean seeds into the milk, discarding the pod. In a bowl, whisk together the eggs and egg yolks and the sugar until the mixture is pale. Whisk the milk mixture into the egg mixture. In the pan cook the mixture over moderately low heat, stirring with a wooden spoon until it registers 175° on a candy thermometer, then strain the custard through a fine sieve into a bowl.

In a small saucepan, whisk together the cornstarch and ¼ cup of the cream to form a thin paste, whisk in the remaining cream and boil the mixture, stirring for 1 minute or until it thickens slightly. Stir the cornstarch mixture, the chocolate mixture and the cocoa powder into the custard and spoon the mixture into fancy stemmed glass or small decorative sauce dishes. Chill overnight. Before serving, spoon a small dollop of whipped cream over top and sprinkle with cocoa powder.

Serves 6-8.

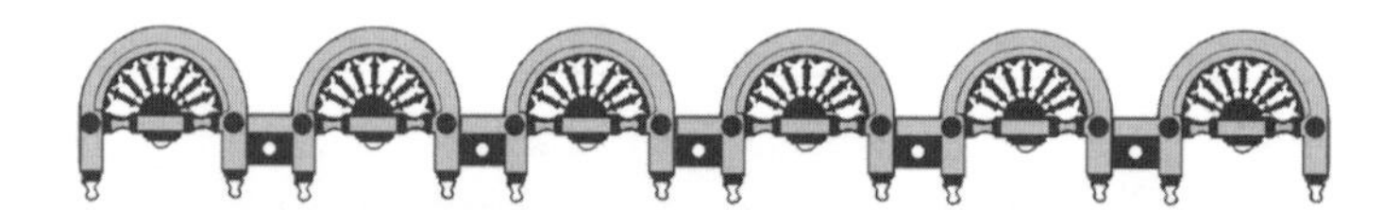

Pastry Cream

¾ cup half and half
½ vanilla bean, cut lengthwise
1 egg
1 egg yolk
¼ cup sugar
1 T flour
½ t cornstarch
½ T unsalted butter

In saucepan, bring half and half and vanilla bean to a boil, stirring constantly. With a whisk or a hand-held electric mixer, beat egg, egg yolk, sugar, flour and cornstarch until lemon-colored and smooth. Pour ¼ of the hot cream into the egg mixture, stirring constantly. Pour egg mixture back into remaining cream and cook over medium heat until mixture boils and becomes smooth and thick, about 1 minute. Whisk in butter. Cover and cool completely. Chill.

Can be used as a filling for your favorite cake or as a filling for tart shells combined with fruit or shaved chocolate.

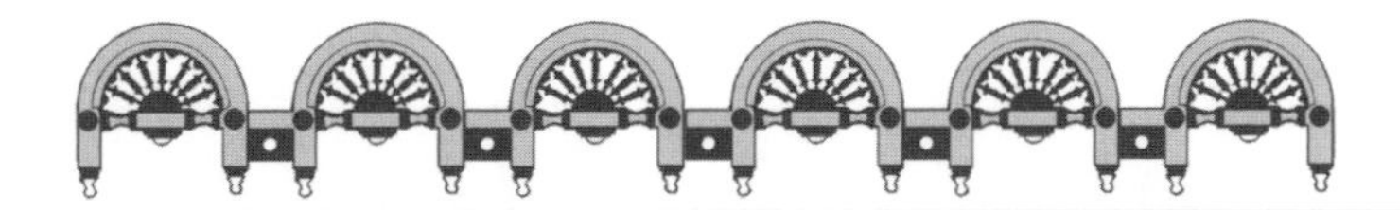

Quick and Easy Custard Filling

½ cup instant vanilla pudding mix
1¼ cup milk
2 T flavoring (raspberry liqueur)
¾ cup heavy cream, whipped stiff

This is a good tart filling recipe when you are pressed for time.

Pour milk and flavoring into pudding mix and mix for 2 minutes until smooth and starting to set. Fold in whipped cream and blend well.

Chill in refrigerator until set.

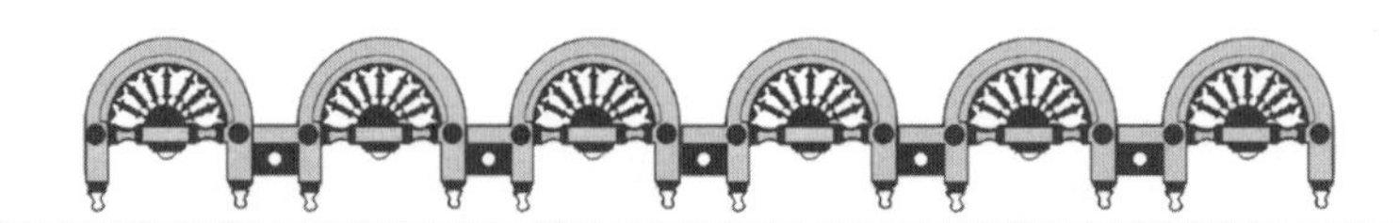

Perfect Pie Crust

This rich flaky pie crust recipe makes enough for 1 double-crust and 1 single-crust 9" pie. You can freeze whatever you have left over.

- 3 cups flour
- 1¼ cup butter-flavored Crisco
- 1 pinch of salt
- 1 egg, slightly beaten
- 1 T cider vinegar
- 5 T cold water

Cut shortening into flour and salt mixture until it resembles a coarse meal.

Mix egg, cider vinegar and cold water thoroughly. Combine with dry ingredients and form into a ball. Wrap and chill for 20-30 minutes before rolling out.

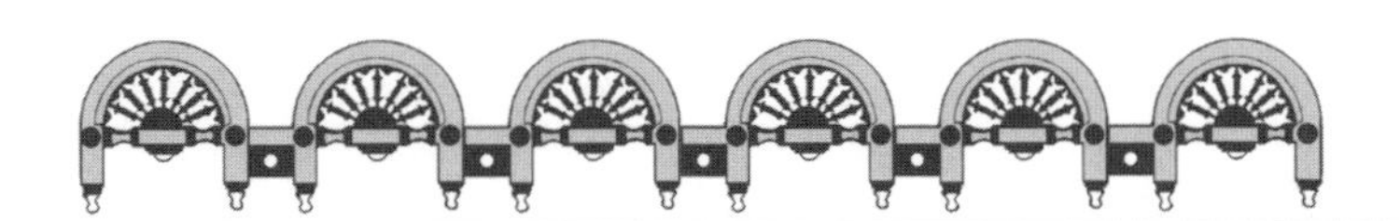

French Raspberry Pie

- 6 cups fresh raspberries
- 1 cup sugar
- ¼ cup quick cooking tapioca
- ½ t cinnamon
- ¼ t salt
- 1 cup sour cream
- 1 unbaked pie shell for a 9" pie. (See perfect pie crust recipe.)

Rinse berries and drain dry. In a small bowl mix sugar, tapioca, cinnamon and salt. Stir in sour cream, let stand 15 minutes to soften tapioca. Put 4½ cups raspberries in to pastry shell reserving the remaining berries for garnish. Pour sour cream mixture evenly over berries in pastry shell.

Bake in 400° oven on lowest rack until filling is bubbly and surface browned, 45 to 55 minutes. Let cool then pile remaining berries on top of pie. Chill. Cut in wedges to serve.

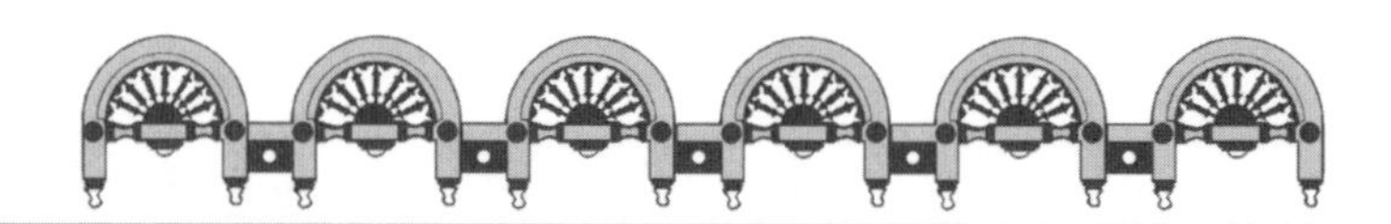

Lou's Favorite Rhubarb Pie

- 4 cups sliced fresh rhubarb
- 4 cups boiling water
- 1½ cups sugar
- 3 T flour
- 1 t quick-cooking tapioca
- 1 egg
- 2 t cold water
- 1 perfect pie crust recipe

Place rhubarb in a colander and pour water over it. Set aside to drain. In a bowl combine the sugar, flour and tapioca, mix well. Add rhubarb and toss to coat. Let stand for 15 minutes. Beat egg and water and add to rhubarb mixture and mix well. Line a 9" pie plate with bottom pastry. Brush bottom with 1 tablespoon sugar and 1 tablespoon flour mixing with fingers to completely cover bottom. This keeps the bottom crust from getting soggy.

Add filling and dot with butter. cover with top pastry and cut off excess and sear edges. Cut slits in top. brush with milk and sprinkle with sugar.

Bake at 400° for 15 minutes. Reduce heat to 350° and bake for 40-50 minutes until browned and filling is bubbly. I always put strips of foil around the edges of my pies while baking so they do not get overly browned, then remove them about the last 15 minutes of baking.

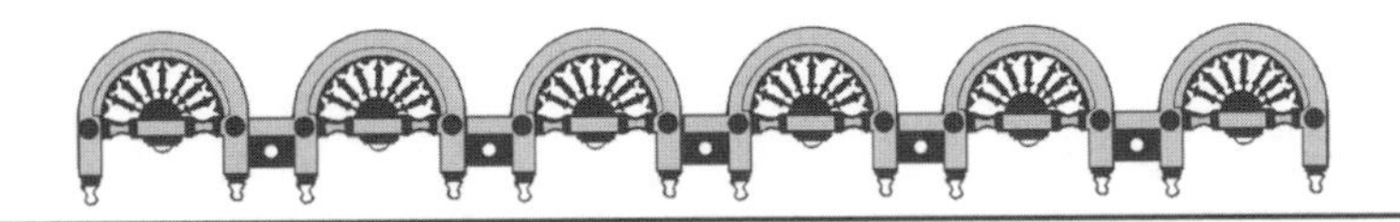

Blue Ribbon Berry Pie

- 6 cups fresh boysenberries, loganberries or blackberries or 8 cups frozen
- 1 cup sugar
- 3 T quick-cooking tapioca
- 1 T flour
- ½ t ground cinnamon
- 1 T lemon juice
- 3 T blackberry flavor liqueur (cordial or brandy)
- 1 perfect pie crust recipe
- 1 deep dish 9″ pie plate or a 10″ pie plate

This recipe makes a large ice cream social-type pie.

In a large bowl stir together sugar, tapioca, cinnamon and nutmeg. Add rinsed and dried berries (if fresh), lemon juice and liqueur. Mix gently. Let stand at least 15 minutes stirring gently now and then. Roll out ½ of pastry dough on floured board and position in the bottom of your pie plate. Sprinkle bottom crust with 1 tablespoon sugar and 1 tablespoon flour and spread this around with your fingers to coat bottom of crust, this will prevent the bottom crust from getting soggy after pie has been cooked.

Fill shell with the prepared berry mixture, dot the top of berries with 1 tablespoon butter cut in small pieces. On floured board, roll out remaining crust. Place over top. Trim off excess and crimp to seal edges. Cut slits in top to let air escape. Brush top lightly with milk and sprinkle with sugar.

Bake in a 375° oven for 55 to 60 minutes or until filling is bubbly and crust is a golden brown. I always put strips of foil around the edges of my pies while baking so they do not get overly browned, then remove them about the last 15 minutes of baking.

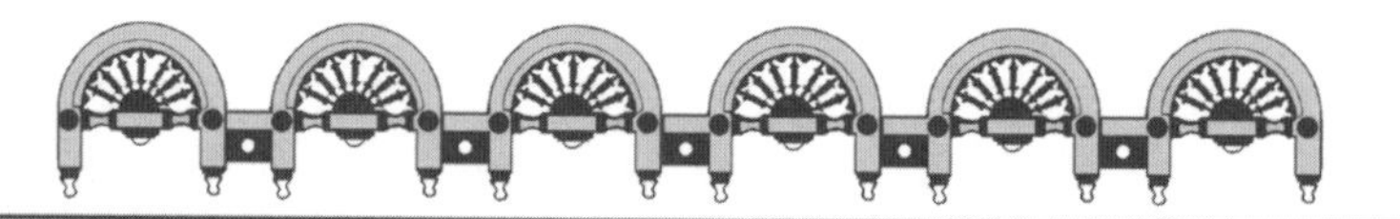

Dora's Lemon Chiffon Pie

Mix sugar and flour. Place boiling water in top pan of double boiler over medium heat in which water in bottom pan is already boiling. Stir in the flour, sugar mixture, stirring constantly until thickened. Then add butter, beaten egg yolks and 1 egg and lemon juice and rind. Cook stirring constantly until thick and custard consistency and mixture coats the back of a wooden spoon. Remove from heat.

Meanwhile, beat egg white until stiff but not dry. Gently fold the white into the lemon mixture and pour into a pre-cooked 9" pie shell. When cool, whip 1 cup of heavy cream with enough sugar to sweeten it and 1 teaspoon vanilla until stiff. Spread over top and garnish top with lemon zest and refrigerate before serving.

1 1/3 cups boiling water
1 cup sugar
1/3 cup lemon juice (fresh)
grated rind of 1 lemon
2 t butter
4 T flour
2 egg yolks (reserve the egg whites)
1 egg
1 cup heavy cream
1 t vanilla
additional sugar

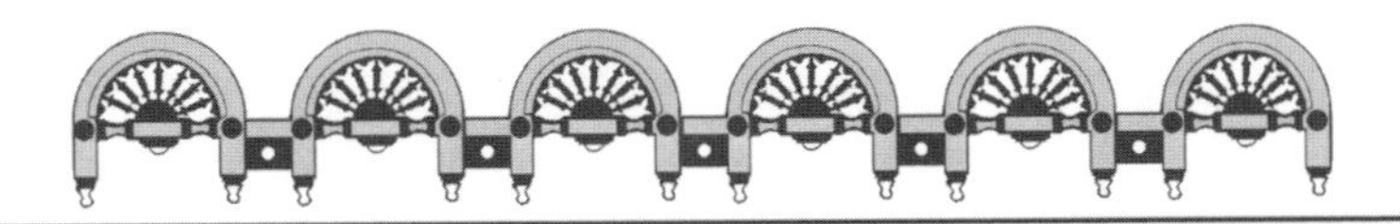

Elsie's Carrot Cake

- 2 cups flour
- 2 t baking powder
- 1½ t baking soda
- 2 t cinnamon
- 1 t salt
- 2 cups sugar
- 1½ cups vegetable oil
- 4 eggs
- 2 cups grated carrots
- 14 oz. crushed pineapple (undrained)
- ½ cup raisins
- ½ cup walnuts coarsely chopped
- Apricot preserves for filling
- 3 9″ cake pans, buttered and dusted with confectioner's sugar or one 9x13″ pan.

Cream Cheese Icing

- 8 oz. cream cheese, softened
- ¼ cup unsalted butter
- 1 lb. confectioner's sugar, sifted
- 2 t vanilla
- half and half

Sift together flour, baking powder, soda, cinnamon and salt. In mixing bowl of electric mixer combine eggs, sugar and vegetable oil just until combined. Add flour while mixer is running then add grated carrots, crushed pineapple, raisins and nuts, and beat just until all ingredients are combined. Divide among the three cake pans and bake at 350° for 30 minutes or until done. Cool completely on wire rack. Remove from pans after 10 minutes.

Cream Cheese Icing

Cream the cheese and butter with an electric mixer. Gradually add confectioner's sugar and vanilla. Thin with half and half to achieve the proper consistency for spreading. Before filling cake, spread a thin coat of apricot jam on each cake layer.

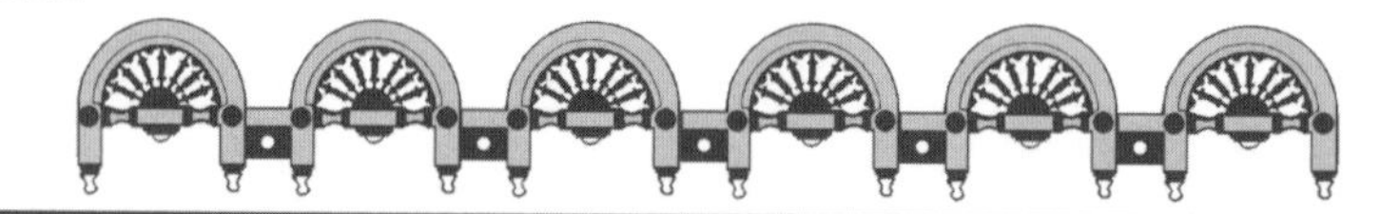

Black Bottom Cupcakes

Filling

Beat cream cheese until fluffy. Add egg, sugar and salt and beat well. Fold in chocolate chips and set aside.

Batter

Beat all ingredients until well blended. Grease mini-cupcake tins well. Pour two thirds of each tin full of batter and add one teaspoon of filling in the center of the batter.

Bake at 350° for 12-15 minutes. Cool on rack for 15 minutes, then turn out of pan to cool completely on rack.

Makes 4 dozen mini cupcakes. Can be kept up to a week in the refrigerator or 2 months in the freezer.

Filling

- 8 oz. cream cheese, softened
- 1 egg
- 1/3 cup sugar
- 1/8 t salt
- 6 oz. package mini chocolate chips

Batter

- 1½ cup sifted all-purpose four
- 1 cup sugar
- 1 cup water
- 1/3 cup vegetable oil
- ¼ cup unsweetened coca powder
- 1 T white vinegar
- 1 t vanilla

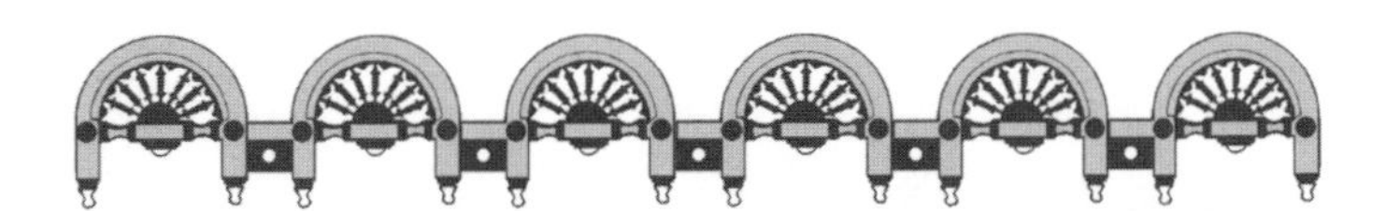

Sour Cream Apple Cake

- 8 T butter, softened
- 2 cups sifted flour
- 1 t baking powder
- 1 t baking soda
- ¼ t salt
- 1 cup sugar
- 2 eggs
- 1 t vanilla
- 1 cup sour cream
- 2 cups peeled and chopped apples (yellow delicious or granny smith)
- 1 t cinnamon
- ¾ cup coarsely chopped pecans
- ½ cup brown sugar
- 3 T melted butter

Sift flour, soda, baking powder and salt. Set aside. Cream butter and sugar until light and fluffy. Add eggs, one at a time and vanilla. Alternately add sour cream and flour mixture. Fold in apples. Pour batter into a greased bundt pan. Mix together cinnamon, pecans, brown sugar and melted butter in a bowl. Sprinkle over the top of the batter.

Bake at 350° for 45 to 50 minutes or until done. When cool, dust with confectioner's sugar.

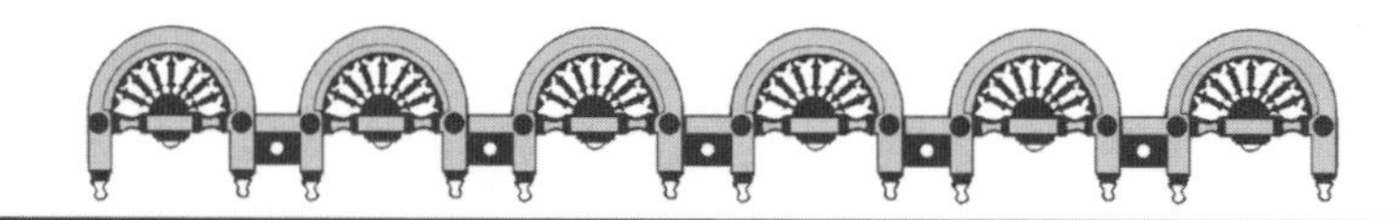

Mom's Chocolate Chip Coffee Cake

Mix flour, salt, sugar, brown sugar, vegetable oil, nuts chocolate chips and coconut together until well combined and measure out ¾ cup of mixture and set aside.

To the remaining mixture add egg, buttermilk, baking soda, nutmeg and cinnamon.

Mix well. Pour batter into a greased and lightly dusted 9x13" pan. Sprinkle reserved ¾ cup coconut, chocolate chip mixture on top. Bake at 350° for 30 minutes. When cool cut into squares.

2 ½ cups flour
1 t salt
¾ cup sugar
1 cup brown sugar
¾ cup vegetable oil
1 cup nuts
1 6 oz. package chocolate chips
1 cup coconut
1 egg
1 cup buttermilk
1 t baking soda
1 t nutmeg
1 t cinnamon

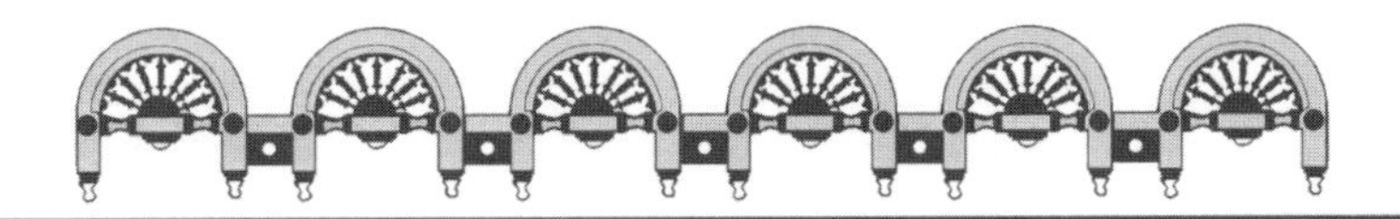

Hazel's Pineapple Nut Cake

½ cup butter
1 cup sugar
4 eggs, well beaten
1½ cups flour
½ t baking soda
1 t baking powder
¼ t salt
1 cup drained crushed pineapple
1 cup chopped walnuts

Pineapple Glaze:
2 T softened butter
1 cup powdered sugar
pineapple

Mix flour, baking soda, baking powder and salt, set aside. Melt butter, add sugar and eggs and mix to combine. Add remaining ingredients and pour into 9x13" baking pan and bake at 300° for 30 minutes. When cool frost with pineapple glaze.

Pineapple Glaze

Use remaining pineapple from a large-sized can (drained). Mix with butter and powdered sugar that have been creamed, and spread over cake.

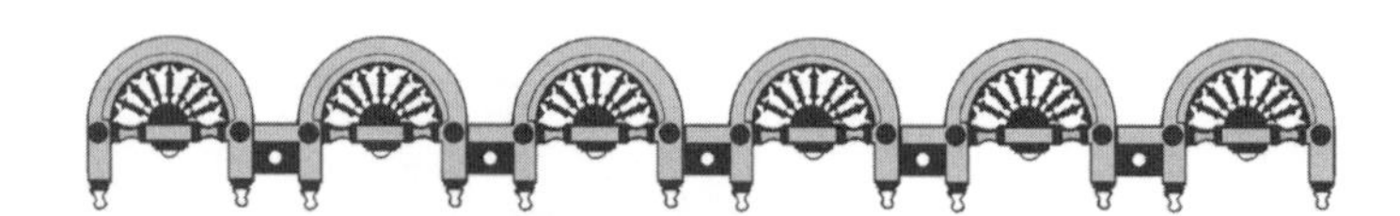

Cake Filling

This is a wonderful filling for any type layer cake.

- 5 T powdered sugar
- 2 eggs, separated
- 1 cup cream
- 1 cup finely chopped nuts
- 1 t vanilla

Beat egg yolks and powdered sugar until thick and pale yellow in color. In separate bowl, beat egg whites until stiff peaks form. In another bowl beat cream and vanilla until thick. Add cream to yolk mixture then fold in whites and chopped nuts. Spread between cake layers.

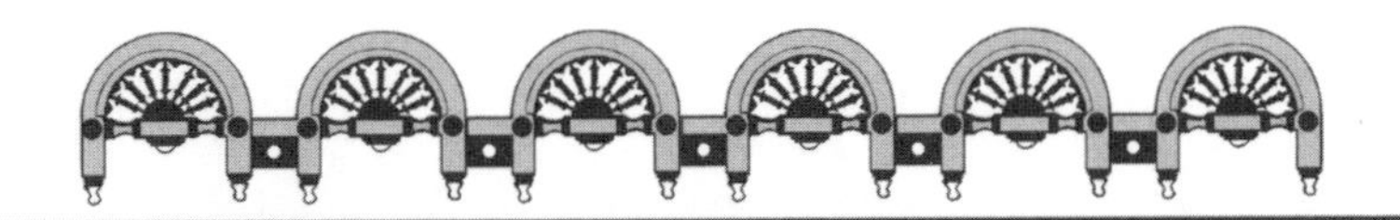

Chocolate Truffle Cake

(A rich fudge-like tea time cake)

16 oz. semi-sweet chocolate
½ cup unsalted butter
1 ½ t flour
1 ½ t sugar
1 t hot water
4 eggs, separated
1 cup whipping cream

Preheat oven to 425°. Grease bottom and sides of an 8" springform pan with butter. Melt chocolate and butter in top of double boiler. Add flour, sugar and water and blend well. Add egg yolks on at a time, beating well after each addition. Beat egg whites until stiff but not dry. Fold into chocolate mixture.

Turn in to pan and bake for 15 minutes only. Cake will look very uncooked in center. Let cool completely. Cake will sink slightly in the middle, then chill. Whip cream until soft peaks form. spread very thin layer over top of cake smoothing with a spatula,

Cut cake while cold but let stand at room temperature about 10 minutes before servings. Serves 8.

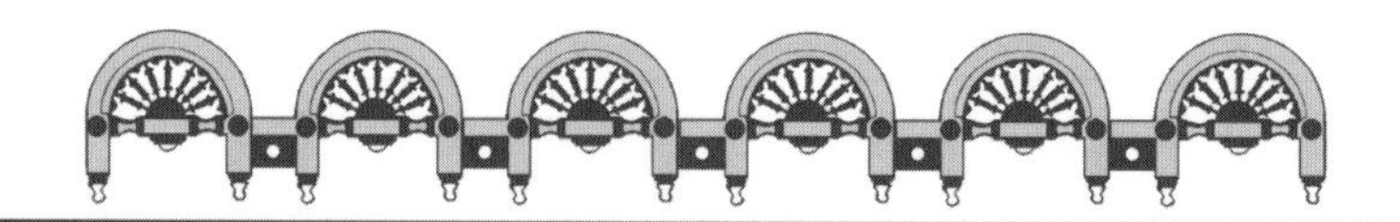

Chocolate Souffle Cake

1 cup unsalted butter
9 oz. bittersweet chocolate
6 eggs-separated
2/3 cup sugar, divided
½ t salt
confectioner's sugar for dusting
fresh raspberries for garnish

Butter and line a 10" spring form with parchment paper and butter parchment.

Melt butter and chocolate over low heat until melted. Remove from heat. Beat together yolks, 1/3 cup sugar and salt until thick and pale, about 6 minutes. Beat whites until just soft peaks begin to form. Gradually add 1/3 cup sugar and beat until stiff peaks just begin to form. Stir chocolate mixture into yolk mixture until well combined. Stir ¼ egg white mixture into chocolate mixture, then fold in remaining egg white mixture gently but thoroughly.

Heat oven to 325° and place a shallow pan of water on bottom rack of oven. This will help give the cake additional moisture as it is cooking. Pour batter into prepared pan and bake on the middle rack of the oven for 1 hour, transfer to rack to cool 10 minutes.

Run knife around edge of pan and remove sides of pan carefully. cool and additional 30 minutes. Invert cake to remove parchment from bottom, then turn right side up again. Transfer to serving plate and dust top with confectioner's sugar and garnish with fresh berries. Serve in narrow wedges.

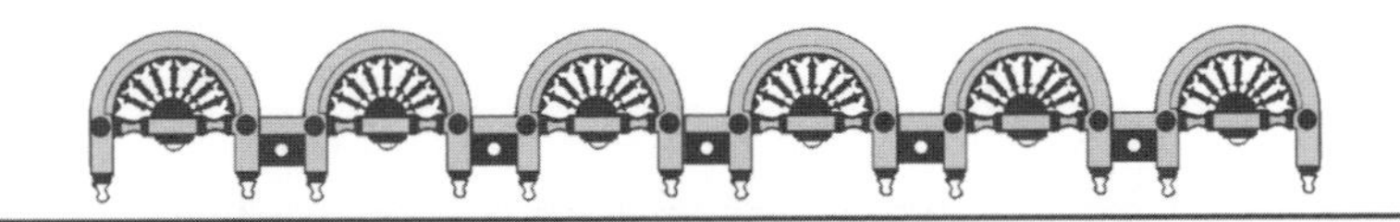

Lemon Blueberry Layer Cake

- 3 cups cake flour
- ½ t salt
- ½ t baking powder
- ½ t baking soda
- ¾ cup unsalted butter, softened
- 2 cups sugar
- ⅓ cup lemon juice
- 1 t grated lemon peel
- 4 large eggs, room temperature, separated
- 1 cup buttermilk
- 2½ cup fresh blueberries

Frosting

- 11 oz. good quality white chocolate, finely chopped
- 12 oz. cream cheese, room temperature
- ¾ cup unsalted butter, room temperature
- 2 T fresh lemon juice

Butter two 9" cake pans with 2" high sides and dust with confectioner's sugar, line bottoms with parchment paper. Sift flour, salt, baking powder and baking soda, set aside. Using large bowl of electric mixer, cream butter until fluffy. Gradually add sugar, beating until blended. Beat in lemon juice and peel then egg yolks, one at a time. Continue to beat until well blended. Beat in dry ingredients in 4 additions. Fold in blueberries.

Beat egg whites until stiff but not dry and gently fold into batter. Divide batter among pans and bake at 350° for 30-40 minutes. Cool cakes in pan on rack. When cool remove from pans and gently peel off parchment paper.

Frosting

Stir white chocolate in top of double boiler. Set over simmering water until almost melted. Remove from over water and stir until smooth. Cool to lukewarm.

Meanwhile, beat cream cheese and butter until blended, light and fluffy. Beat in lemon juice then cooled white chocolate. Cake can be garnished with fresh blueberries.

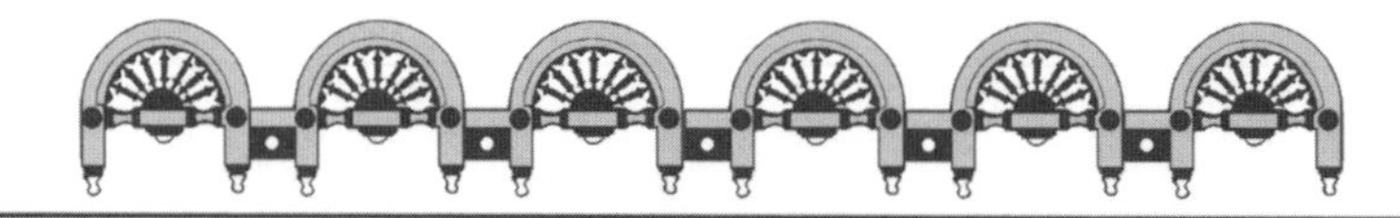

Perfect Chocolate Cake

Cake

In medium bowl combine cocoa with boiling water and mix with wire whisk until smooth. Cool completely. Sift flour with soda, salt and baking powder. Preheat oven to 350°, grease and lightly flour three 9x1½" layer cake pans.

In large bowl of mixer, at high speed, beat butter, sugar, eggs and vanilla until light and fluffy, about 5 minutes, scraping bowl occasionally. At low speed, beat in flour mixture (in fourths) alternately with cocoa mixture (in thirds) beginning and ending with flour mixture. Be careful not to over beat.

Divide evenly into prepared pans. Bake 25-30 minutes or until centers spring back when gently pressed. Cool in pans 10 minutes. Carefully loosen sides on pan with a knife and remove form pan and cool completely on racks.

Frosting

In medium saucepan combine the chocolate pieces, cream, butter; stir over medium heat until smooth. Remove from heat. With whisk blend in 2½ cups confectioner's sugar. In a bowl set over ice water beat until it holds shape and becomes spreadable.

Filling

Whip cream with sugar and vanilla, refrigerate. Assemble on plate, place a layer top side down. Spread with half of the cram. Place second layer top side down. Spread with the rest of cream. Frost cake beginning with the sides. Refrigerate at least 1 hour before serving.

Cake

1 cup unsifted unsweetened cocoa
2 cups boiling water
2¾ cups sifted all-purpose flour
2 t baking soda
½ t salt
½ t baking powder
1 cup unsalted butter, softened
2½ cups sugar
4 eggs, room temperature
1½ t vanilla extract

Frosting

1 6 oz. package semi-sweet chocolate pieces
½ cup light cream
1 cup unsalted butter
2½ cups unsifted confectioner's sugar

Filling

1 cup heavy cream, chilled
¼ cup unsifted confectioner's sugar
1 t vanilla extract

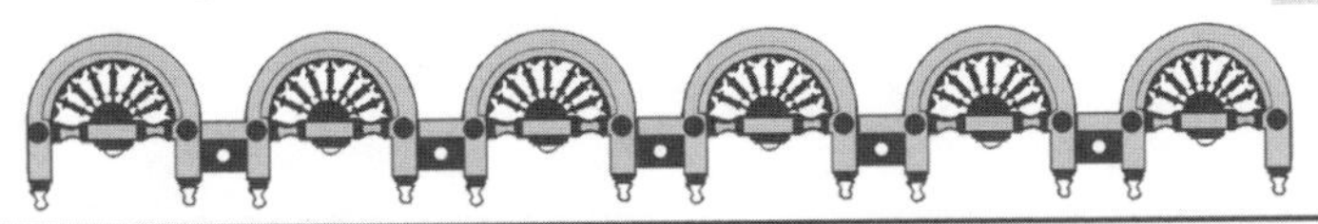

Classic Vanilla Layer Cake with Whipped Cream Frosting

Cake
¾ lb. softened unsalted butter
3 cups sugar
9 large eggs, separated
1½ t vanilla
3 cups cake flour
1½ t baking powder
¾ t baking soda
¾ t salt
1½ cups buttermilk

Frosting
4 T flour
1 cup milk
½ cup butter
½ cup shortening
1 cup sugar
2 t vanilla
1-2 cups sifted powdered sugar

Cake

Butter two deep (3-4") 9" cake pans or 3 regular 9" cake pans and set aside. In bowl of electric mixer, cream butter, Add the sugar a little at a time and beat the mixture until light and fluffy. Beat in the egg yolks, one at a time and the vanilla. Into a bowl, sift the cake flour, baking powder, baking soda and salt.

In another bowl, with electric mixer beat the whites until they just hold their shape. Add the dry ingredients and buttermilk alternately into the butter mixture. Do not over beat. Fold in the egg whites. Divide the batter between the two pans. Bake for 35 to 40 minutes in a 350° oven or until tester inserted in center comes out clean. When cool, frost with whipped cream frosting.

Frosting

A very good, never-fail white icing that is great for piping and decorating.

Mix flour and milk in saucepan. Cook over low heat until thick. Cool.

Cream butter and shortening in bowl of electric mixer for 4 minutes. Add 1 cup of sugar and beat 4 minutes longer. Add flour paste and beat 4 minutes more. Add vanilla and enough of the powdered sugar to make a stiff icing, blend until combined well.

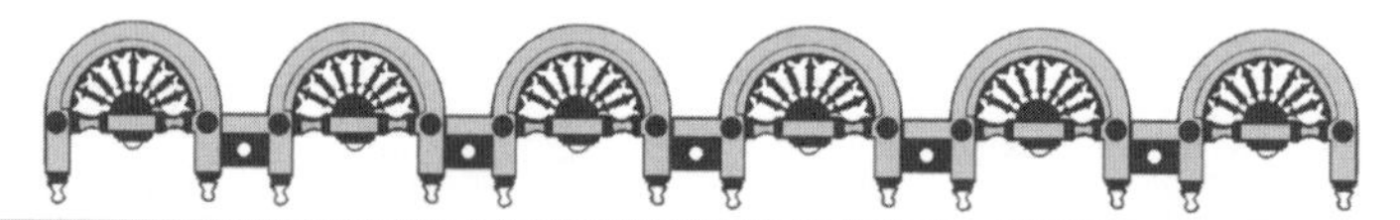

Prune Cake with Buttermilk Vanilla Sauce

Cake

Sift together flour, baking powder, baking soda, salt and spices. Set aside.

In a large bowl combine sugar, oil, eggs, vanilla and buttermilk until blended. Stir in flour mixture and beat until all ingredients are well incorporated. Fold in prunes. Pour into well greased bundt pan and bake at 300° for 1 hour or until done.

Buttermilk Vanilla Sauce

Heat ingredients in double boiler until warm and combined. Pour over slightly warm cake.

Cake
2 cups sugar
¾ cup oil
3 eggs beaten
1 t vanilla
1 cup buttermilk
2 cups flour
1 t baking powder
1 t baking soda
½ t salt
1 t cinnamon
1 t nutmeg
1 t allspice
1 cup pitted prunes, chopped fine

Buttermilk Vanilla Sauce
½ cup sugar
¼ cup buttermilk
½ cup butter
1 t vanilla

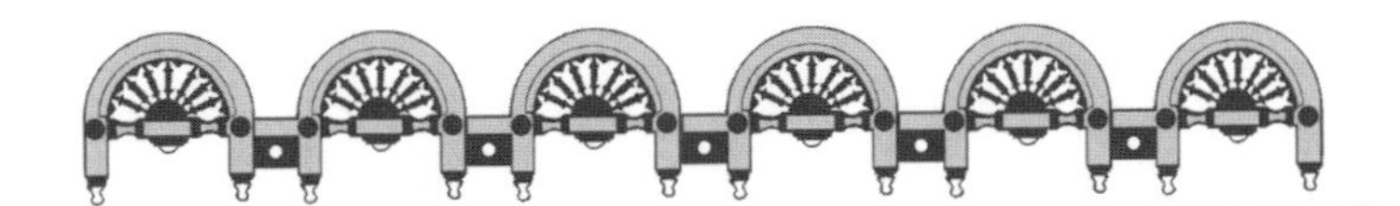

Apple-Mincemeat Cake

3 cups flour
4 t baking powder
1 t cinnamon
1 t ground ginger
½ t allspice
½ t salt
1 cup vegetable oil
½ cup butter, melted and cooled
1½ cups firmly packed dark brown sugar
3 eggs lightly beaten
1½ grated apples, granny smith or red rome
1½ cups mincemeat, preferably homemade
½ cup chopped walnuts or pecans
1 t vanilla
whipped cream or confectioner's sugar

Preheat oven to 350°. Grease a 10" bundt pan very well. In a medium bowl, combine flour, baking powder, spices and salt and mix well. Set aside. In a large bowl of electric mixer, combine oil, butter and brown sugar and beat until smooth. Beat the flour mixture into the sugar mixture, adding a third of the flour mixture at a time and beating until smooth after each addition. Beat in the eggs one at a time. Stir in the grated apples, mincemeat, nuts and vanilla.

Pour batter into prepared pan and bake for 1 hour or until done. Turn warm cake out onto a serving platter an serve with unsweetened whipped cream immediately, or cool completely and dust with powdered sugar.

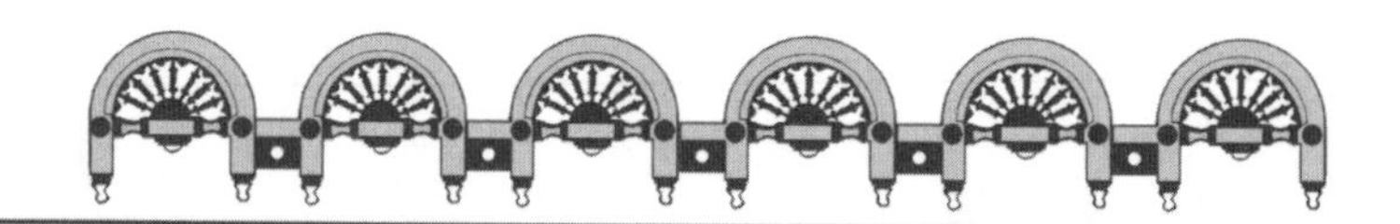

Old-Fashioned Mincemeat

(for canning)

1 venison neck (about 5 lbs.)
1½ T salt
¼ t white pepper
½ cup cider vinegar
2½ lbs. beef suet
10 lbs. apples (preferably Bellflower, but Granny Smith will do)
½ gallon apple cider
3½ lbs. sugar (white)
½ T allspice
½ of a fifth of Brandy
1½ lbs. brown sugar
1 pint molasses
1½ lbs. mixed diced candied fruit (glazed cake fruit)
5 lbs. raisins
2½ lbs. dried currants
½ T mace
1 T cinnamon
2 fresh nutmegs, grated
½ of a fifth of dark rum

Place neck in a large kettle with just enough water to cover. Add salt, pepper and vinegar. Cook meat over low heat until tender and beginning to pull away from bone. Remove membrane from suet and grind up. Peel and dice apples very fine. Remove meat from liquid reserving the liquid. Chop the meat up in very fine pieces. Add the apples and the suet to the meat liquid and cook for 20 minutes. Then add ½ the cider, meat, sugars, molasses, candied fruit, spices and remaining cider, raisins and currants.

Cook until suet is transparent and raisins are plump (about 2 hours), stirring often. Pour the run into the cooked mincemeat, stirring vigorously. Fill sterilized quart-size mason jars to one inch of top. Add 1 tablespoon brandy and seal quickly.

Process in a water bath for 30 minutes. To use mincemeat, remove from jar and run through a meat grinder or gently pulse in a food processor. Pour a little additional brandy in the mincemeat and stir well before using for a pie or tarts.

I have included a number of recipes in this book using mincemeat. This mincemeat is the "best."

Yields 12 quarts.

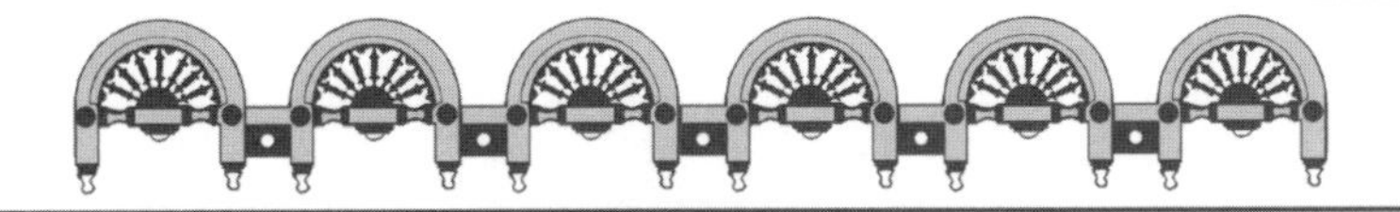

Double Chocolate Layer Cake

Cake

3 oz. fine quality semi-sweet chocolate
1½ cups hot brewed coffee
3 cups sugar
2½ cups flour
1½ cups unsweetened cocoa powder
2 t baking soda
¾ t baking powder
1¼ t salt
3 large eggs
¾ cup vegetable oil
1½ cups buttermilk
¾ t vanilla

Rich Chocolate Icing

24 oz. semisweet chocolate chips
4 cups whipping cream
1 t light corn syrup

Cake

Preheat oven to 300° and butter 2 10x2" round cake pans and line the bottoms of each pan with parchment paper and butter the paper. Finely chop chocolate and add to a bowl together with the hot coffee. Let mixture stand, stirring occasionally until chocolate is melted and the mixture is smooth.

Into a large bowl stir together sugar, flour, cocoa powder, baking soda, baking powder and salt. In another bowl with of an electric mixer beat eggs until thickened slightly and lemon colored, about 3 minutes. Slowly add oil, buttermilk and melted chocolate mixture to eggs, beating until well combined. Add sugar, flour mixture and beat on medium speed just until well combined.

Divide batter between the prepared pans and bake until done or tester inserted in the center comes out clean (about 1 hour).

Cool completely in pans on a rack. When cool, loosen edges with knife and invert layers onto rack. Carefully remove parchment paper. Frost with rich chocolate icing.

Rich Chocolate Icing

Place chocolate and cream in heavy saucepan. cook over low heat stirring constantly until combined and thickened, about 20 minutes. Increase heat to medium low and cook 3 minutes more stirring constantly. Remove from heat and stir in corn syrup. Transfer to a large metal bowl and refrigerate. Check about every 15 minutes and stir. Do this until the mixture is cool enough to spread, about 2 hours.

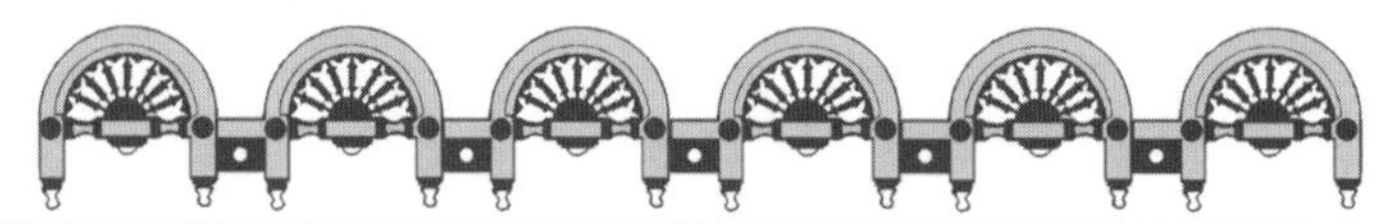

Walnut Rum-Raisin Cake

Cake
1 cup golden raisins
½ cup dark rum
2½ cups sifted flour
2 t baking powder
1 t baking soda
¼ t salt
¼ t nutmeg
1 cup unsalted butter, softened
1 t vanilla
1 cup sugar
2 eggs
1 cup buttermilk
1 T grated lemon peel
1 T grated orange peel
2 cups chopped walnuts
confectioner's sugar

Rum Sauce
½ cups sugar
¼ cup water
2 T orange juice
2 T lemon juice
2 T dark rum

Cake

In bowl, combine raisins and rum. Cover and soak overnight or several hours.

Sift flour with baking powder, baking soda, salt and nutmeg. Set aside. In a large bowl of electric mixer, beat butter until light and fluffy. Add the vanilla and sugar and beat until mixed. Beat in eggs. With mixer on low speed, add dry ingredients in 3 additions, alternating with buttermilk. Stir in lemon and orange peels, raisins and walnuts. Pour into greased and floured bundt pan. Bake at 350° for 50 minutes or until done. Cool in pan 10 minutes.

Turn cake out onto serving plate and using a wide pastry brush, brush warm Rum Sauce over warm cake. Cool. Sprinkle with confectioners sugar before serving.

Rum Sauce

In small saucepan, combine, sugar and water. Bring to a boil over medium heat. Boil 2 minutes, remove from heat and cool slightly. Stir in orange and lemon juices and rum.

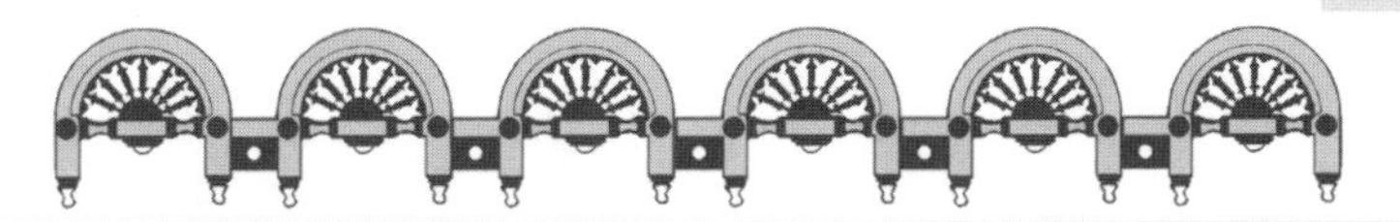

Pumpkin Log

3 eggs beaten on high for 5 minutes
1 cup sugar
¾ cup pumpkin
1 t baking powder
¾ cup flour
1 t ginger
2 t cinnamon
1 cup nuts, chopped
½ t salt
½ t nutmeg
1 t lemon juice
powdered sugar

Filling
1 cup powdered sugar
½ t vanilla
6 oz. cream cheese
2 T butter

Beat eggs 5 minutes on high, beat in sugar, pumpkin, lemon juice. Add sifted dry ingredients. Mix. Spread in jelly roll pan 11x17x1". Pour nuts over top. Bake 15 minutes at 375°. Sprinkle dish towel with powdered sugar. Cool in pan 5 minutes. Drop out onto towel. Rollup cloth and all tightly until cool. Unroll and spread with filling.

Filling

Beat together until smooth. Spread on cake and re-roll and wrap in foil, refrigerate. Serves 16.

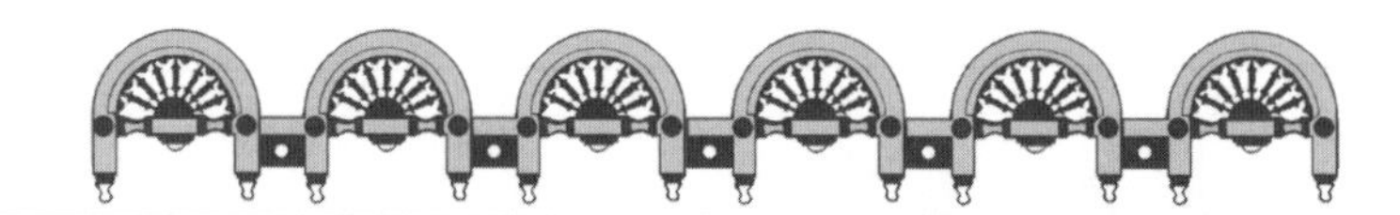

May's Apple Torte

A quick and easy, but very tasty dessert.

- 2 eggs beaten well
- ½ t salt
- 1½ cups sugar
- 3 t vanilla
- ⅔ cups flour
- 2 t baking powder
- 2 cups apples (granny smith or yellow delicious), peeled and diced
- 1 cup chopped walnuts

Mix all ingredients together and pour into a greased 9x12" baking dish. Bake at 350° for 30 minutes. Serve with whipped cream or ice cream.

Serves 6.

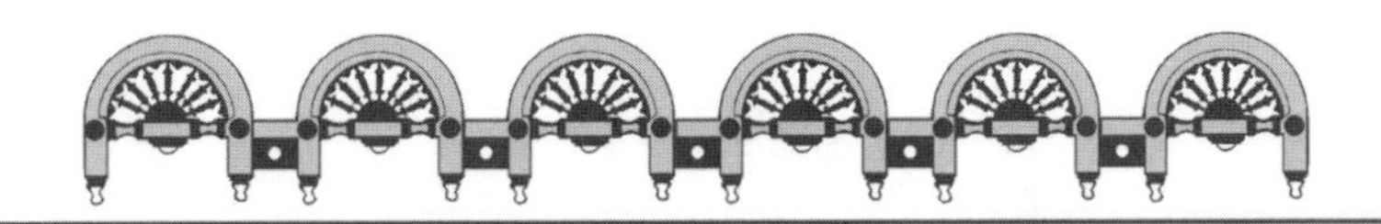

Mini Butterhorns

1 cup butter, softened
2 cups flour
12 oz. cottage cheese

Mix ingredients in electric mixer until smooth. Form into ball and wrap and refrigerate overnight. Divide dough into 3 parts. Roll each section out into an 8" round on a floured surface. Cut each section into 12 wedges. Roll up starting with wide end. Bake on a lightly greased baking sheet for 30 minutes at 325°.

When cool, glaze with confectioner's sugar that has been mixed with a little lemon juice.

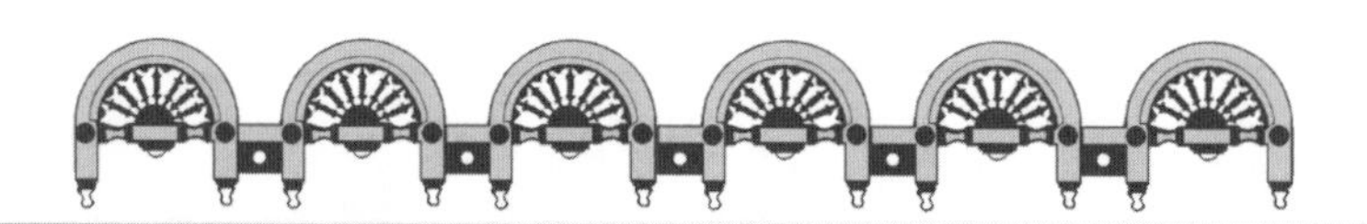

Chocolate Raspberry Cheesecake Napoleons

Thaw cheesecake in refrigerator overnight. Soak raspberries in liqueur for 1 hour or up to 3 hours, then drain well. Thaw, cut and bake puff pastry sheets according to Mini Napoleon directions on package (enough to serve 8). Whip cream to stiff consistency. In a medium-sized mixing bowl of electric mixer, beat cheesecake unto broken up and crumbly. Add 1/3 of whipped cream and beat until smooth. Do not over beat. Set aside.

- 1 package Frozen Pepperidge Farms Puff Pastry Sheets
- 1 16 oz. jar Hershey's Chocolate Shoppe Fudge topping (hot fudge)
- 1 frozen gourmet quality New York style cheesecake (21 oz.-6" round)
- 1 pint heavy whipping cream
- 1 cup raspberry liqueur (optional)
- 2 baskets fresh raspberries or frozen raspberries
- powdered sugar for dusting

Assembly

Spread 8 bottom pastry layers with a thin coat of chocolate topping. Next, spread a layer of cheesecake mixture followed by a layer of raspberries then a thin layer of whipped cream. Add another pastry layer and repeat the process. Add a third layer of pastry and top with a dollop of whipped cream, a couple of raspberries and a dusting of powdered sugar.

Serves 8.

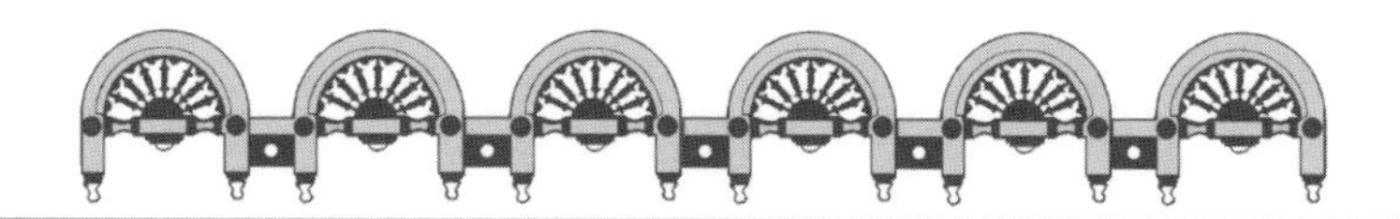

Lemon Spice Puffs

- ¼ cup warm water 105° to 115°
- 1 package active dry yeast
- 1 cup warm milk, 105° to 115°
- ½ cup sugar
- 5 T unsalted butter, softened
- 2 T poppy seed
- 1 T grated lemon peel
- 1 t salt
- 3 cups all-purpose flour
- 2 eggs
- 2 t nutmeg

Place warm water in large warm bowl. Sprinkle in yeast, stir until dissolved. Stir in warm milk, 6 tablespoons sugar, butter, poppy seed, lemon peel, salt and 2 cups flour, blend well. Add eggs and remaining flour stirring until smooth. Cover and let rise in warm spot until double in bulk, about 1 hour. Stir batter down.

Grease 24 mini-muffin pan cups. Spoon batter into cups filling half full. In small bowl combine remaining 2 tablespoons sugar and nutmeg. Sprinkle evenly over each cup. Cover and let rise for about 30-35 minutes until doubled.

Bake at 375° for 20 minutes. Remove from cups and cool on a wire rack.

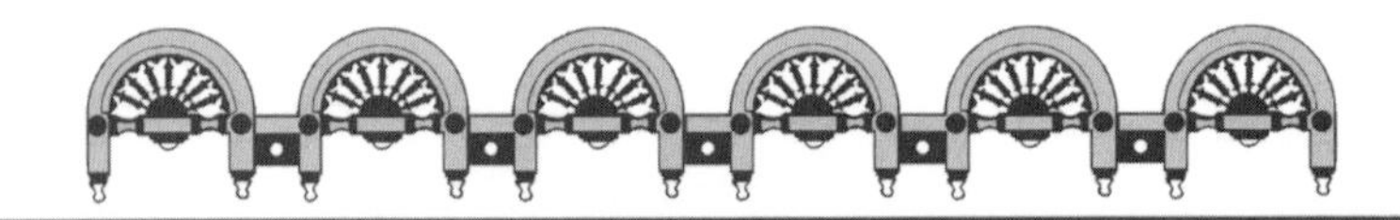

Steamed Persimmon Pudding

(A Holiday Favorite)

2 t baking soda
1 cup pureed persimmons (about 3 peeled persimmons)
½ cup unsalted butter, softened
1 ½ cups sugar
2 eggs
1 T lemon juice
2 T rum
1 cup flour
1 t cinnamon
½ t salt
1 cup chopped walnuts or pecans
1 cup raisins

In a small bowl, stir baking soda into persimmon puree. Set aside.

In bowl of electric mixer, cream butter and sugar. Add eggs, lemon juice and rum and beat well. Add flour, cinnamon, salt and persimmon mixture. Beat until well combined. Stir in nuts and raisins. Spoon batter into greased 2 quart pudding mold. Cover tightly with lid or foil. Place on rack in large pot with enough boiling water to come half way up the sides of the mold and steam for 2 hours. Remove from kettle and let rest for 5 minutes. Turn onto rack to cool or cool just slightly and serve warm. Can be reheated covered in the oven to serve later with hard sauce.

Serves 8.

Hard Sauce

⅓ cup butter, softened
1 cup confectioners sugar
1 t rum or brandy
1 T hot water

In a bowl, cream butter until light and fluffy. Gradually add sugar and cream and beat to combine. Beat in rum, stirring constantly. Add hot water gradually to prevent curdling. Beat until fluffy. Spoon sauce into a small serving dish and refrigerate until cold.

Serve with warm steamed pudding.

Makes ¾ cup.

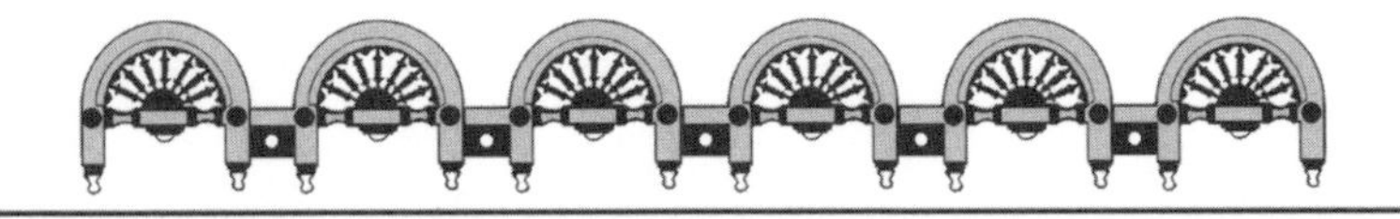

Blueberry Scones

4 cups flour
3 T sugar
4 t baking powder
½ t salt
½ t cream of tartar
⅔ cup butter
1 large egg
1½ cups half & half
1½ cups fresh or unthawed
frozen blueberries
Additional sugar for topping

Heat oven to 400°. Grease two large baking sheets. In large bowl, combine flour, sugar, baking powder, salt and cream of tartar. With pastry blender, cut in butter until mixture resembles coarse crumbs.

Separate egg, placing egg white in cup and yolk in a small bowl. With fork, beat egg yolk, stir in half & half. Add yolk mixture to dry ingredients and mix lightly with fork until mixture clings together and forms a soft dough. Turn dough out onto lightly floured surface and knead gently several times. Gently knead in blueberries. Divide dough in half; pat out each half into an 8" round, and cut each into 8 wedges.

Place scones on greased sheet. Pierce tops with a fork. Brush with reserved egg white and sprinkle with sugar. Bake 15-18 minutes, or until golden brown.

Note: May substitute another type of berry or raisins or currants. Mixture of brown sugar, cinnamon and nuts may be sprinkled on top of raisin or currant scones, if desired.

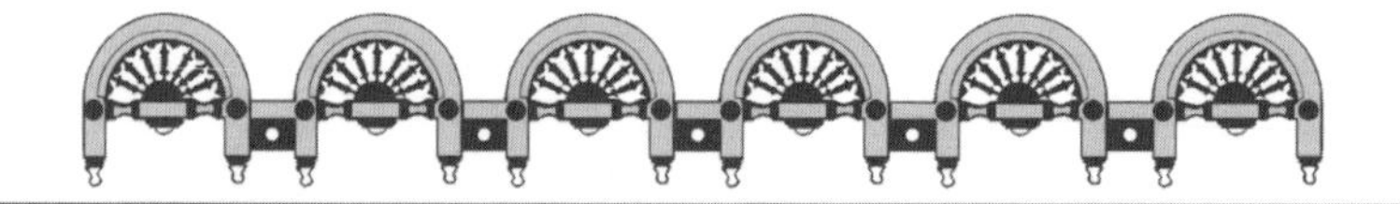

Orange Currant Scones

- ½ cup currants
- 1 cup boiling water
- 2 cups flour
- 3 T sugar
- 2 T baking powder
- 1 t baking soda
- 1 t salt
- Grated peel of 1 orange
- 5 T butter
- 1 egg, separated
- 1 cup sour cream

Soak currants in boiling water. Set aside.

Add dry ingredients to bowl. Cut in butter. Drain currants and add to dry mix. Mix egg yolk with sour cream and add to dry mix. Blend until mixture holds together. Turn out on floured board and knead several times, then flatten out and cut with cookie cutter.

Place on greased sheet. Brush tops with beaten egg white and sprinkle with additional sugar. Bake 375° for 15 minutes or until lightly browned.

Makes 12-15 scones.

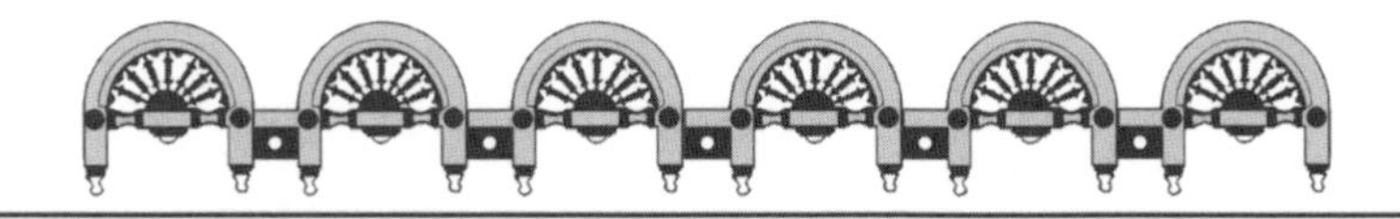

Cheddar Cheese Scones

2 cups flour
1 T baking powder
½ t onion salt
1 T dried parsley
¼ cup butter, cold
1 cup shredded sharp cheddar cheese
1 egg
½ cup half & half
Extra half & half for brushing on top

Combine dry ingredients. Cut in butter. Stir in cheese and mix until well combined. Add egg and cream that have been mixed together.

Knead for 1 minute. Roll out into a circle and cut into wedges. Brush with additional half & half and place on a greased baking sheet.

Bake for 12 minutes or until golden brown in a 425° oven.

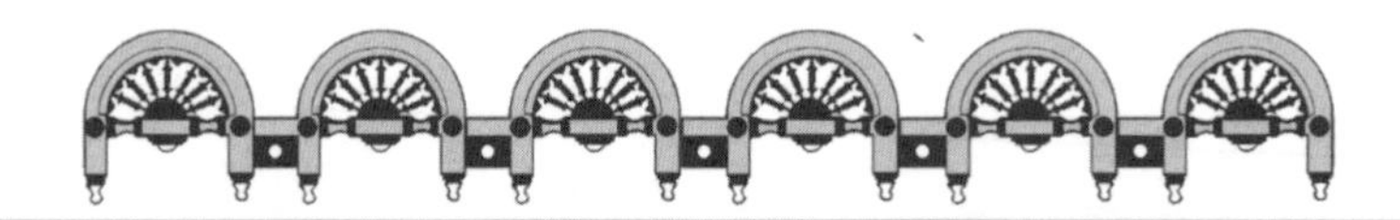

Cheese and Herb Scones

Rich and savory, these scones are a meal in themselves

- 4 cups flour
- 4 t baking powder
- 1 t salt
- ½ t dried basil
- ¼ t dried thyme
- ¼ t ground red pepper
- ⅔ cup vegetable shortening
- 1 cup shredded cheddar cheese
- 1⅓ cups milk
- 1 T Dijon mustard

In large bowl, combine flour, baking powder, salt, basil, thyme and red pepper. With pastry blender cut in shortening until mixture resembles coarse meal. Stir in ¾ cup cheese. Add milk and mustard to the mixture and blend lightly with a fork until the mixture holds together and forms a soft dough.

Turn out onto a lightly floured surface and knead gently 5 or 6 times. Divide dough in half and press each half into a 9" round. Cut each into 6 wedges. Place scones 1" apart on a greased baking sheet. Prick tops with a fork and brush with water and sprinkle with remaining cheese.

Bake for 15 to 18 minutes at 400°. Serve warm.

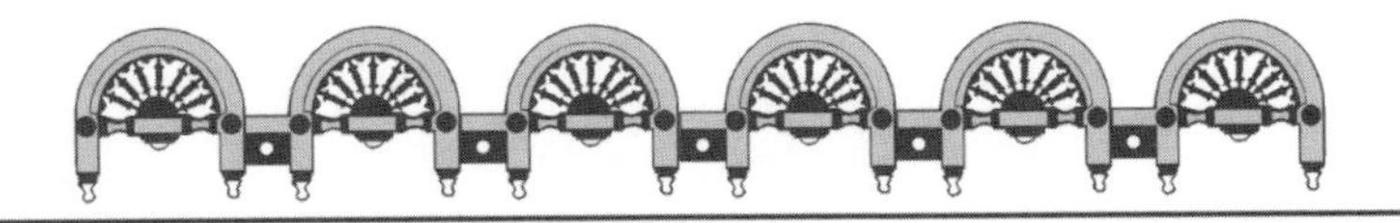

Gingerbread Scones

- 4 cups flour
- 3 T brown sugar
- 4 t baking powder
- ½ t salt
- ½ t cream of tartar
- 2 t ginger
- 1 t cinnamon
- ¾ cup butter
- 1 large egg
- ⅓ cup molasses
- ¾ cup half & half
- ½ cup pumpkin
- Additional brown sugar and pecans for topping

Heat oven to 400°. Grease 2 baking sheets (approximately 13x15"). In large bowl, combine flour, sugar, baking powder, salt, cream of tartar and spices. With pastry blender, cut in butter until mixture resembles coarse crumbs. Separate egg, placing egg white in a cup and beat slightly, set aside. Place egg yolk in medium bowl and beat with a fork. Stir in molasses, pumpkin and half & half; add yolk mixture to dry ingredients and mix lightly with fork until mixture clings together and forms a soft dough.

Turn dough out on lightly floured board and knead gently several times. Divide dough in half; pat each half out into 8" rounds. Brush with egg white and sprinkle with reserved brown sugar and chopped pecans. Cut each round into 8 wedges. Place on greased baking sheet and bake 15-18 minutes or until golden brown.

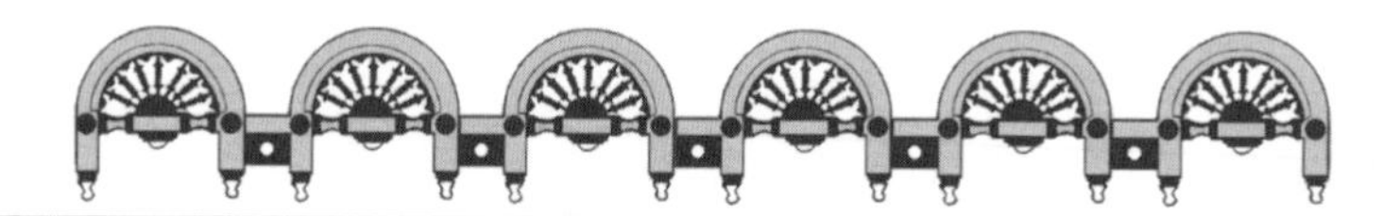

Petits Fours

- 1 pound cake recipe (recipe follows)
- chocolate fudge icing (home-made or ready-made)
- raspberry preserves

Bake pound cake in two parchment-lined jelly roll pans (11x15") at 350° for 30 minutes.

When cool, frost one cake top with a ¼-inch thick layer of chocolate fudge icing, followed by a thin layer of raspberry preserves. Invert second cake on top of frosted cake, forming a sandwich. Press the two layers gently together. Cover with foil and freeze for several hours.

Cut frozen cake into 1-inch squares. Dip into melted chocolate and transfer to wire rack to set.

Additional tinted white chocolate may be piped on top of each petit four with a fanciful design of stripes.

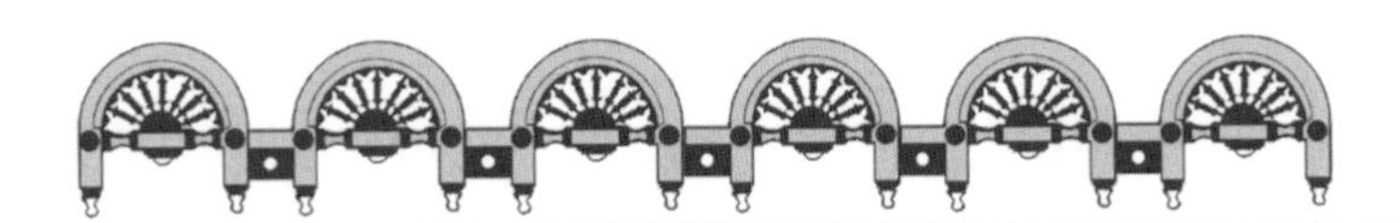

Sour Cream Pound Cake

- 1½ cups butter
- 2½ cups unbleached flour
- 2½ cups sugar
- ½ t salt
- 5 eggs
- ½ t baking soda
- 1 t vanilla
- 1 cup sour cream
- 1 t almond extract

Cream butter until fluffy. Gradually add sugar, ½ cup at a time. After sugar has been added and mixture is very light and fluffy, add eggs, one at a time and vanilla and almond extract. In a separate bowl, sift together the flour, salt and baking soda. Add the flour mixture to the butter-sugar-egg mixture alternately with the sour cream.

Pour the batter into 2 greased 5x9" baking pans. Bake for 1 hour at 350°.

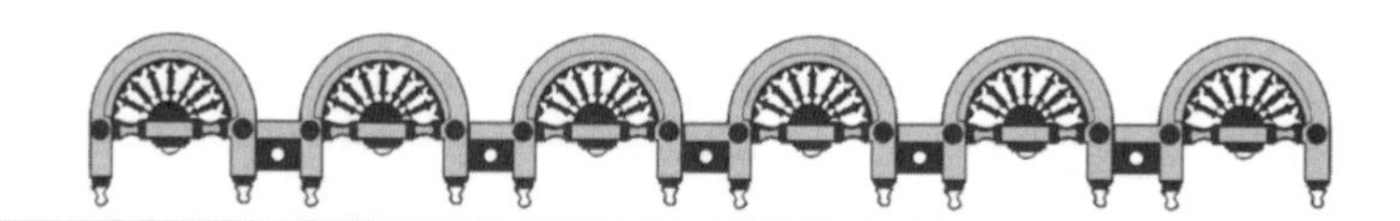

Lemon-Filbert Pound Cake

1 cups unsalted butter
2¾ cups sugar
6 eggs
3 cups flour
½ t salt
¼ t baking soda
1 cup lemon yogurt
½ t vanilla
½ t grated lemon peel
½ cup chopped filberts,
pecans can also be used
powdered sugar

Grease and flour two 8x4x2" loaf pans. In large mixing bowl beat butter at medium speed until creamy and fluffy, 3 minutes. Gradually add sugar a little at a time beating about 13 minutes or until fluffy and sugar is dissolved. Add eggs, one at a time, beating about one minute after each, scraping bowl often. Beat two more minutes.

Mix flour, salt and soda. Combine yogurt, vanilla and lemon peel. Add flour and yogurt mixtures alternately to creamed mixture, beat just until well blended. Fold in nuts.

Divide batter between prepared pans. Bake at 375 ° for 1¼ to 1½ hours.

Cool in pans 15 minutes. Remove and cool on racks. When cool sprinkle with powdered sugar.

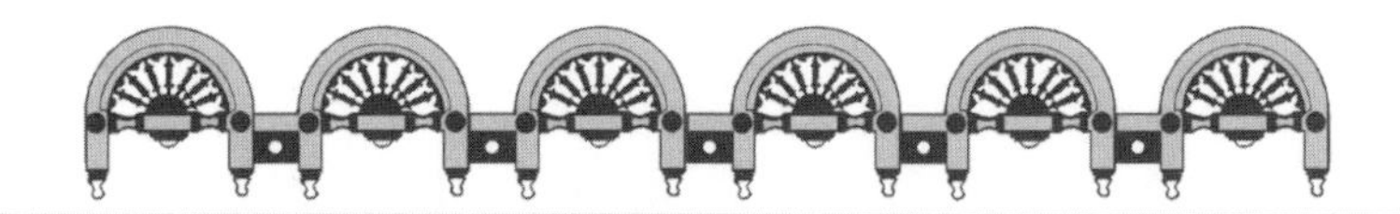

Marmalade Tea Bread

- 1 cup unsalted butter, softened
- 1½ cups sugar
- 4 eggs
- 3 cups cake flour
- 1 t salt
- ¾ t cream of tartar
- ½ t baking soda
- ½ cup sour cream
- 1 cup orange marmalade (preferably English)
- ½ cup golden raisins

Marmalade Sauce

- ½ cup orange marmalade (preferably English)
- ¼ cup orange juice
- ½ t lemon juice
- ⅛ cup sweet sherry

Cream butter until light and fluffy. Add sugar gradually and beat until fluffy, scrapping the bowl often. Add the eggs one at a time, beating well after each addition. Sift dry ingredients and set aside.

Combine the sour cream and marmalade in a separate bowl. Add the dry ingredients and marmalade mixture alternately to the butter mixture, then fold in the raisins.

Bake in two greased loaf pans at 350° for 1 hour. Pour the marmalade sauce over the bread while still warm and in the pans.

Cool completely before removing from pans. Wrap tightly and store in the refrigerator or freezer.

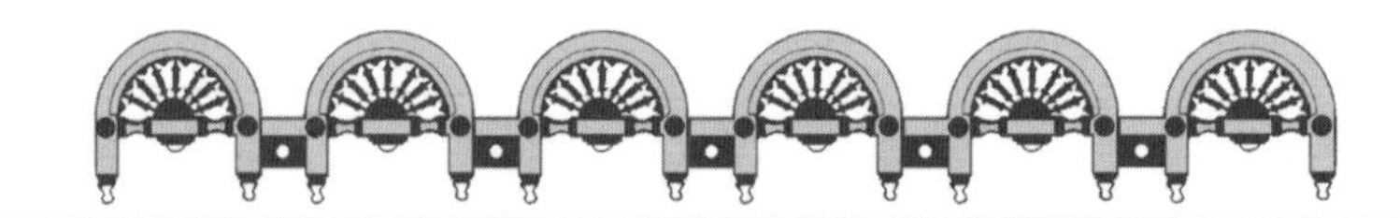

Harvest Apple Cake

Combine the apples, eggs and oil in a mixing bowl. In another bowl, combine the flour, sugar, salt, baking soda and cinnamon. Stir the flour mixture into the apples and mix well. Thoroughly oil two 5x9" loaf pans. Coat the pans with a sugar/cinnamon mixture. Pour the batter into the pans and bake at 350° for 60 minutes.

- 2½ cups unpeeled apples, chopped and cored (yellow delicious or Granny Smith)
- 3 eggs beaten
- 1 cup oil
- 2 cups all-purpose flour
- 2 cups sugar
- 1 t salt
- 1½ t baking soda
- 1 t cinnamon
- extra cinnamon and sugar

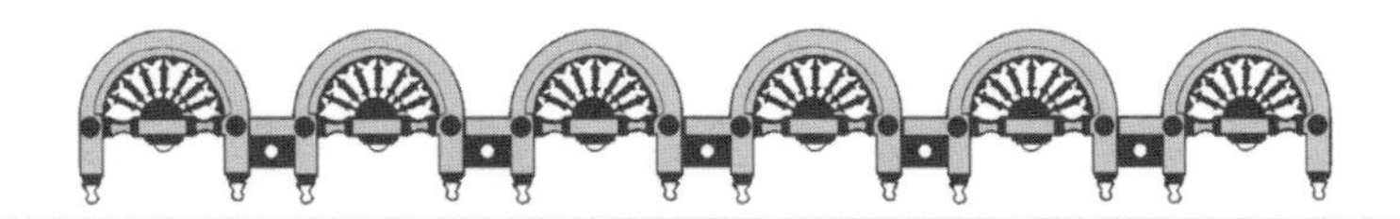

Pumpkin Gingerbread

(A favorite at tea time)

- 3 cups sugar
- 1 cup vegetable oil
- 4 eggs
- 3½ cups flour
- 1 t baking soda
- 1½ t salt
- ½ t baking powder
- 2 t ginger
- 1 t cinnamon
- 1 t nutmeg
- 1 t cloves
- 1 t allspice
- 16 oz. can pumpkin
- ⅔ cup water

Sift together all dry ingredients except sugar. In a bowl of electric mixer, cream sugar, oil and eggs until light and fluffy. Alternately add flour mixture and water to egg mixture. Blend in pumpkin and beat until well mixed. Pour into 2 greased 5x9" loaf pans and bake at 350° for 1 hour.

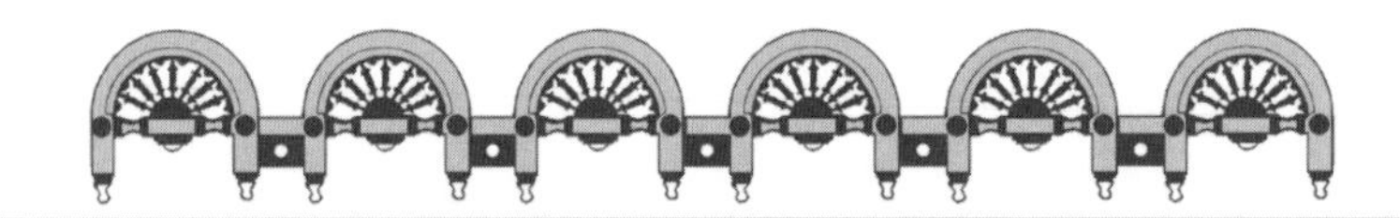

Poppy Seed Bread

Heat oven to 350°. Generously grease two 9x5x3 inch loaf pans.

Combine first 5 ingredients and mix on medium speed of an electric mixer until well blended. Sift together flour, baking powder and salt. Blend into egg mixture on low speed. Add poppy seed and vanilla and beat until smooth. Turn into pans and bake until done, about 1 hour.

- 2½ cups sugar
- 2½ cups cooking oil
- 2 cups evaporated milk
- 5 eggs
- ½ cup milk
- 5 cups flour
- 4½ t baking powder
- ¼ t salt
- ½ cup poppy seed
- 2½ t vanilla

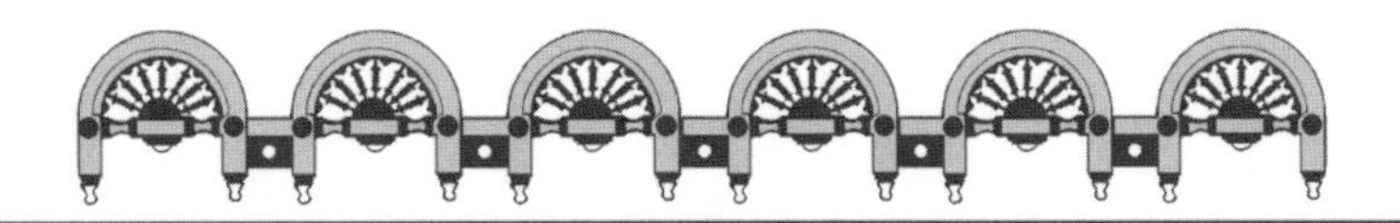

Sour Cream Banana Bread

- 2 cups sugar
- 4 eggs
- 1 cup butter (2 sticks) softened
- 2 t vanilla
- 3 cups flour
- 2 t baking soda
- 1 t salt
- 2 cups ripe bananas, mashed
- 1 cup sour cream
- ¾ cup chopped walnuts

Whisk together flour, baking soda and salt. In electric mixer bowl cream together butter and sugar until light and fluffy. Add eggs 1 at a time, beating well after each addition. Add vanilla. Add dry ingredients and mix until blended. Add bananas, nuts and sour cream. Mix thoroughly and pour into 2 greased 5x9" loaf pans. Bake at 350° for 1 hour.

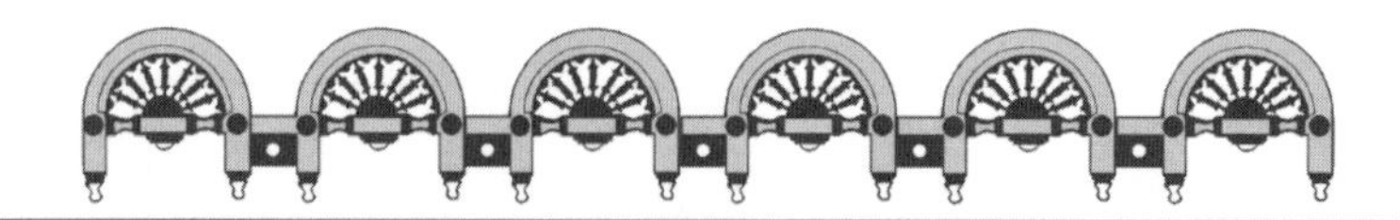

Gingerbread Mansion Very Lemony Lemon Bread

½ cup butter
½ cup milk
1 cup sugar
½ cup finely chopped nuts
grated lemon peel
2 eggs, slightly beaten
1¼ cups flour
1 t baking powder
½ t salt

Topping
⅛ cup sugar
juice of one lemon

Sift flour with baking powder and salt. Cream butter and sugar. Mix in eggs. Alternately add flour mixture and milk, stirring constantly. Mix in nuts and lemon peel. Bake in a greased 5x9" loaf pan for about 50 minutes or until done when tested. Bake at 350°. As soon as bread comes out of oven, poke holes in the top with fork and spoon over the topping of sugar and lemon juice.

Note: Mix the topping just prior to use or it will not be smooth.

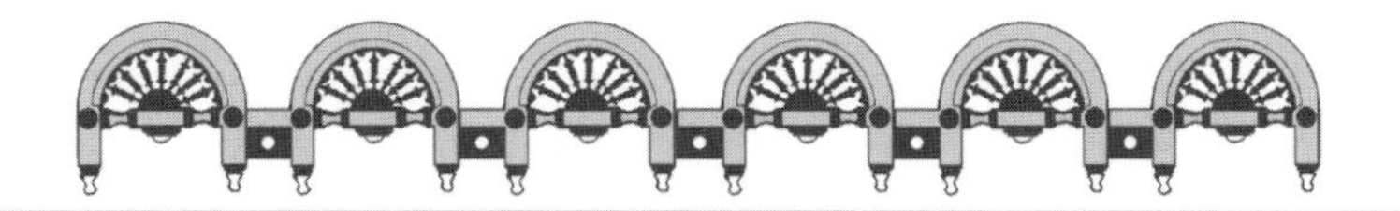

Heavenly Zucchini Bread

3 eggs
1 t vanilla
2 cups sugar
¾ cup oil
3 small bananas, sliced
3 cups flour
1 t salt
2 t baking soda
2 t cocoa
2 t cinnamon
2 cups unpeeled grated zucchini
1 cup chopped nuts
1 cup raisins or dates, chopped

Beat together eggs, vanilla, sugar, oil and bananas.

Sift together flour, salt, baking soda, cocoa and cinnamon. Stir well into banana mixture. Add zucchini, nuts and raisins or dates.

Pour into 2 5x9" loaf pans. Bake at 350° for 1 hour.

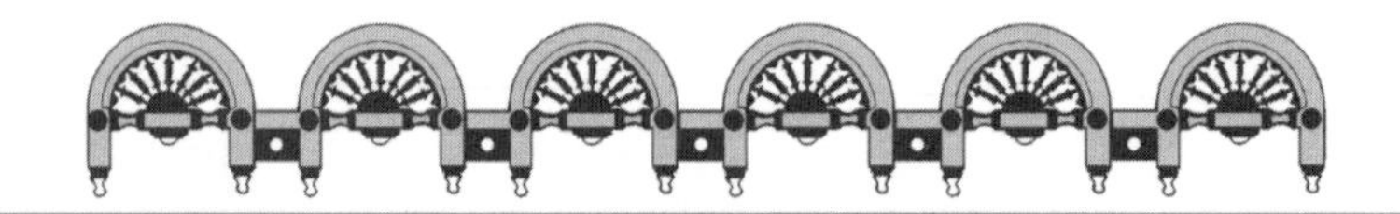

Brandied Fruitcake

(dark and rich)

- 2 lb. candied cherries
- 2 lb. candied pineapple
- ½ lb. candied orange peel
- ½ lb. candied lemon peel
- 1 ½ lb. pecans
- 1 ½ lb. pitted dates
- 2 lb. golden raisins
- 1 lb. dark raisins
- 1 lb. currants
- 1 lb. butter
- 1 lb. brown sugar
- 1 cup molasses
- 1 dozen large eggs
- 3 t vanilla
- juice of 1 large lemon
- juice of 1 large orange
- 4 cups sifted flour
- 4 t baking powder
- 1 t nutmeg
- 1 t allspice
- 1 t cinnamon
- 1 t cloves
- 1 t mace
- 2 cups grape jelly
- 1 cup Brandy

Dice candied fruits and peels. Chop nuts into coarse pieces and snip dates into smaller pieces with scissors dipped into hot water. Combine fruits and nuts into large bowl and toss with enough additional flour to coat well. Cream butter and brown sugar until light and fluffy, about 3 minutes. Add eggs one at a time beating well after each addition. Mix in molasses and beat well. Stir in vanilla, lemon and orange juices. Sift together flour, baking powder and spices. Beat together jelly and Brandy until smooth.

Alternately, add flour mixture and jelly to creamed mixture, blending well. Stir in fruit and nut mixture. Dough will be very stiff. Butter 6-8 loaf pans 5x9" size and line with parchment paper or cut up brown paper bags and butter the paper. Fill pans ¾ full of batter and smooth tops.

Bake at 300° until tester inserted in the center comes out clean, about 2½ hours. Cool cakes in pan. Remove caked from pans and peel off paper. When completely cool, pour a little brandy over the top and wrap each loaf in Brandy soaked cheesecloth, then wrap in foil. Store in a cool place. These fruit cakes need to sit for at least 3 months to ripen before eating. Twice each month unwrap the foil from the fruit cakes and pour a little brandy over each one, being careful to wrap them up tightly again with the foil.

It has taken me a long time to perfect this recipe and I really cherish it, but I feel it's time to share it. I make my fruitcakes in September so they will be ready for the holiday season. Also, it is a good idea to buy the candied fruit you will need at holiday time for the following year. In our area there is no candied fruit to be found in September.

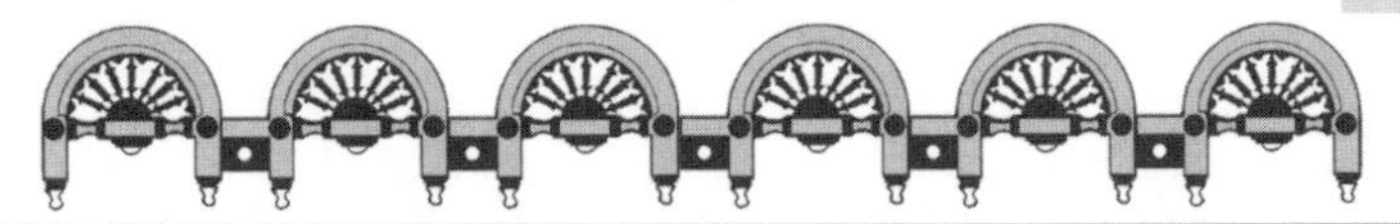

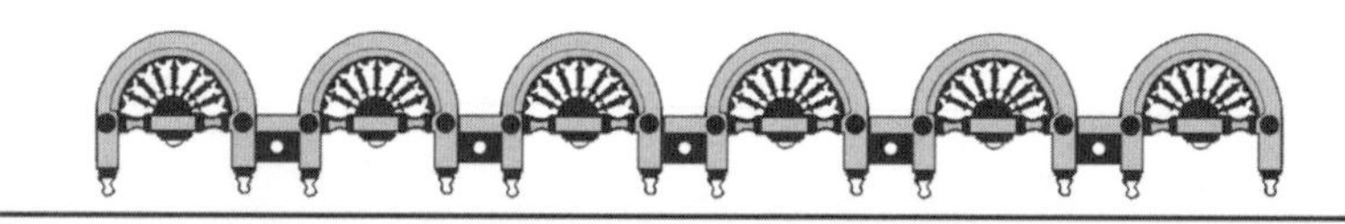

Savory Delights: Dips, Sandwiches, Tarts, Spreads

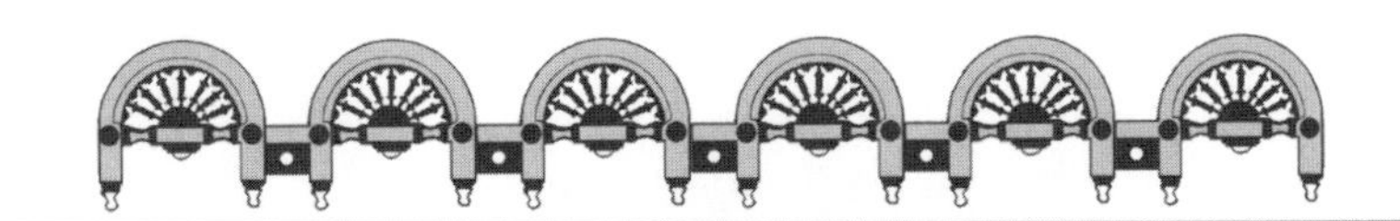

Tea Time Cheese Ball

8 oz. cream cheese, softened
5 oz. Cheddar Cheese Spread, softened
10 oz. Blue cheese
1 small onion, minced
1 garlic clove, minced
2 T brandy or dry sherry
Toasted chopped nuts for coating

Beat cheeses until well blended and fluffy. Add remaining ingredients and mix well. Chill in refrigerator for 1 hour. Roll in ball, then roll in toasted nuts to coat. Chill until ready to use.

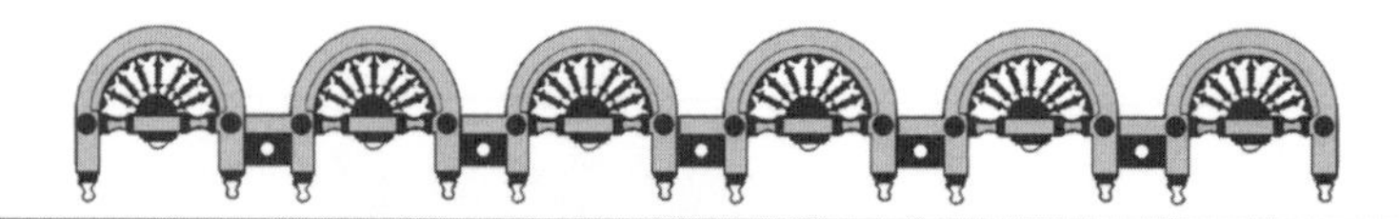

Teatime Fruit Dip

Combine all ingredients until well blended. Serve with fresh strawberries, and apple and pear slices.

1 cup peach preserves
¼ t nutmeg
¼ t finely chopped fresh ginger or
⅛ t ground ginger
2 cups sour cream

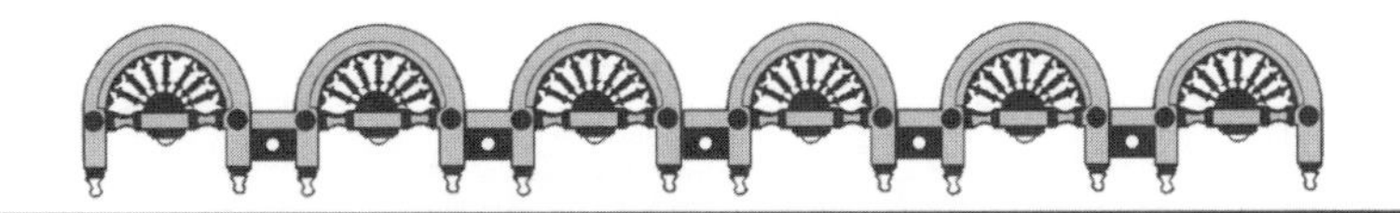

Three Cheese Dip

1 cup cottage cheese, drained
½ cup sharp Cheddar cheese, grated
½ oz. blue cheese, crumbled
1 T mayonnaise
1 T horseradish
½ T Grey Poupon mustard
2 green onions, finely chopped
pinch of salt and pepper

Combine all ingredients. Serve with sliced apples and pears, or with crackers.

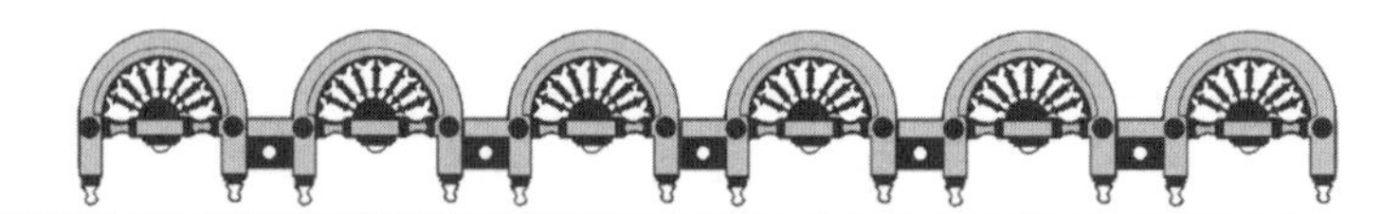

Devonshire Cream #1

Beat cream until stiff adding sugar just as cream thickens. Fold in sour cream. Chill. Serve at tea time as an accompaniment to scones and jam.

½ cup heavy cream
2 T confectioners sugar
½ cup sour cream

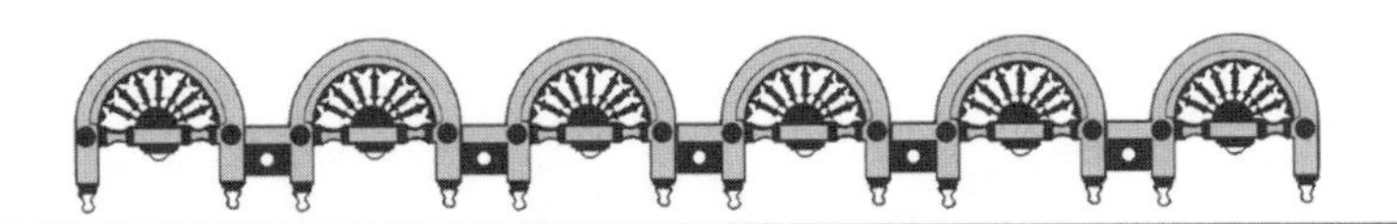

Devonshire Cream #2

8 oz. cream cheese, softened
½ cup sour cream
2 T confectioners sugar

Beat cream cheese until fluffy. Add sour cream and sugar and beat until smooth. Serve with jam as an accompaniment to scones at tea time.

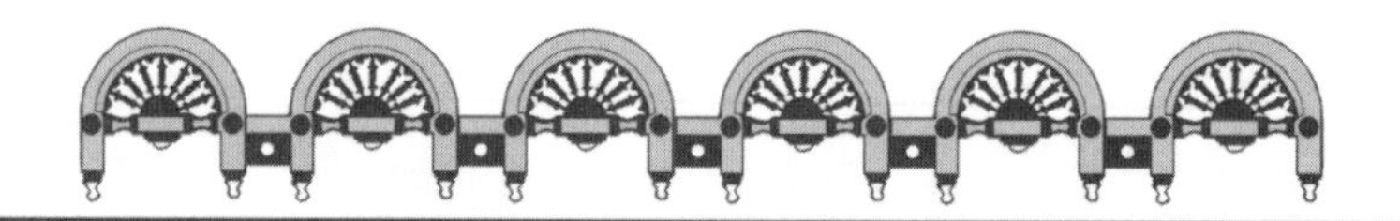

Raspberry Tea Sandwiches

1 8 oz. package cream cheese, softened
3 T raspberry preserves
½ cup fresh raspberries
fresh mint leaves
16 slices white bread

Remove crusts from bread and cut out into desired shapes with cookie cutter. In a small bowl of electric mixer, combine cream cheese and raspberry preserves. Spread a thin layer of the mixture on each sandwich cut out. Garnish with fresh raspberries and mint.

Will make 3 to 4 dozen sandwiches.

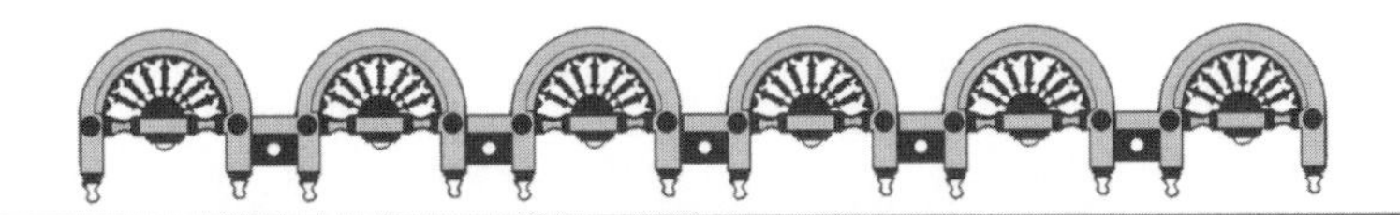

Curry Tea Sandwiches

1 8 oz. package cream cheese, softened
¼ cup orange marmalade
1 t curry powder
½ cup flaked coconut
thinly sliced green onions
chopped roasted peanuts
raisins
16 slices white or brown bread, crust removed

Cut bread into desired shapes with a cookie cutter.

Combine cream cheese, orange marmalade and curry. Spread mixture lightly onto bread cut outs. Sprinkle a little coconut, peanuts, green onions and a couple of raisins on top of each sandwich.

Makes 30-40 sandwiches.

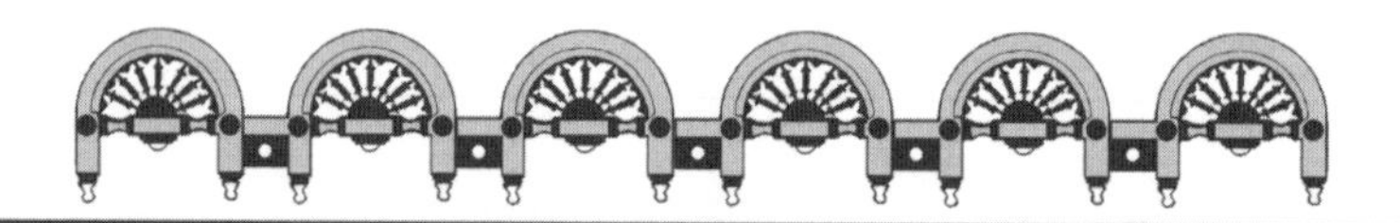

Cucumber Sandwiches

3 T prepared horseradish
1 cup heavy cream
1 cucumber
bread, white and brown
salt and pepper

Whip cream until stiff. Fold in horseradish carefully. Peel cucumber and slice very thin. Spread one white piece of bread with whipped cream mixture. Arrange 4 cucumber slices on top. Sprinkle with salt and pepper. Spread a brown piece of bread with whipped cream mixture and put on top. Press down gently to secure the two slices. Cut off crusts and cut into triangle shapes. Stand on end to serve.

Sometimes I add thinly-sliced Roma tomatoes along with the cucumbers.

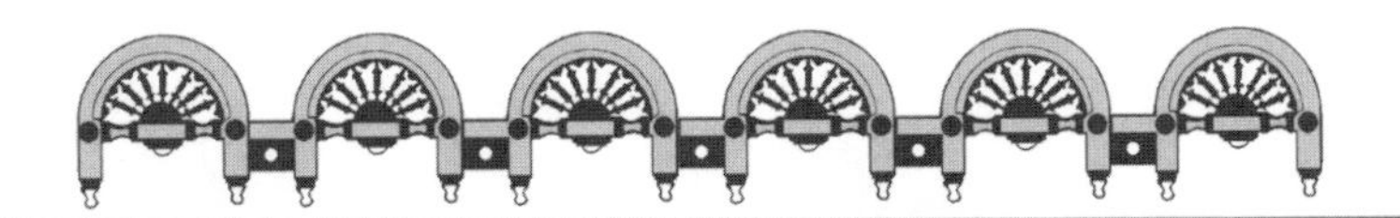

Fruit and Veggie Sandwiches on Raisin Bread

- 2 8 oz. packages cream cheese, softened
- 1 8 oz. can crushed pineapple, drained
- 1/3 cup orange marmalade
- 3 T ginger preserves or 1 t ground ginger
- ½ cup finely chopped pecans
- ¼ cup finely chopped red bell pepper
- 1 T minced onions
- ½ t celery salt
- ½ t onion salt

Mix all ingredients well in the bowl of an electric mixer. Spread on a layer of raisin bread. Top with another piece of bread and press gently to secure slices of bread. Trim off crust and cut into triangle shapes. Cover with a damp cloth and chill until ready to serve.

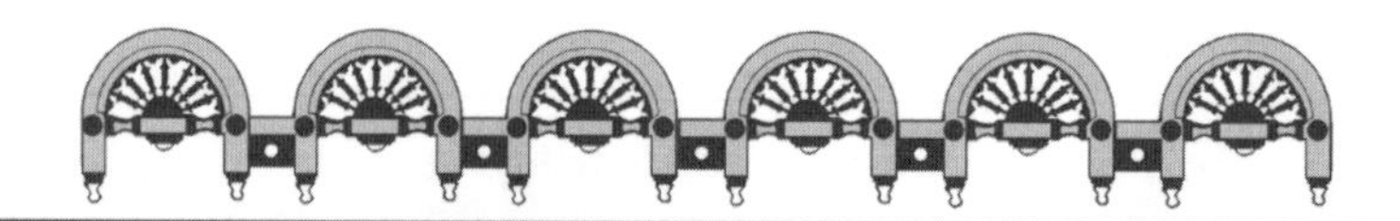

Pineapple, Sweet Red Pepper and Mint Sandwich Filling

- 1 8 oz. package cream cheese, softened
- ¼ cup well-drained crushed pineapple
- 1 T minced red bell pepper
- 1 T fresh pineapple mint or spearmint

Beat cream cheese until light and fluffy. Add crushed pineapple, bell pepper and mint and mix well to combine. Chill.

Spread on lightly buttered bread in which crust has been removed. Cut each piece of bread into four triangle shapes.

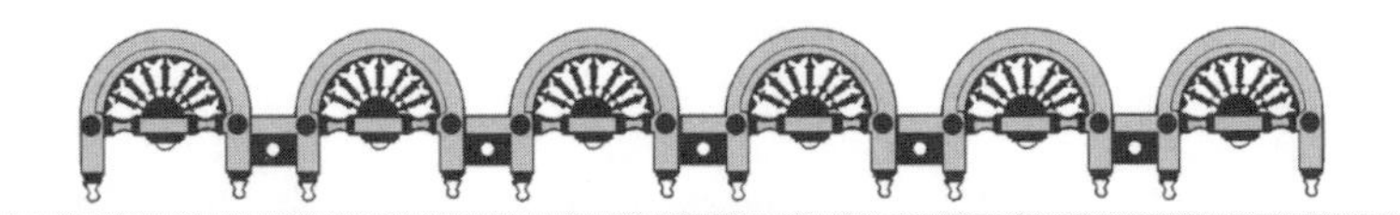

Cucumber and Tomato Tea Sandwiches

1 cube plus 2 T unsalted butter, softened
1 t dry mustard
½ t freshly ground pepper
½ t salt
¾ t fresh lemon juice
3 T minced fresh coriander
1 large tomato
1 cucumber, peeled
8 slices white bread
8 slices whole wheat bread

A classic tea-time savory...

In small bowl, combine butter, mustard, salt, pepper, lemon juice and coriander. Blend well. Thinly slice the tomato and drain on paper towels. Peel the cucumber and cut off ends. Cut into 3" sections. Thinly slice each piece lengthwise.

Spread the flavored butter on one side of each bread slice. Arrange the tomato slices in a single layer on 4 slices and the cucumber in a single layer on 4 slices. Cover each sandwich with the remaining 8 buttered slices of bread and press gently together.

Using a sharp serrated knife, trim off sides to remove crust. Quarter each sandwich diagonally to make into 4 little triangles. Lay on wax paper lined sheet and cover with a damp tea towel and refrigerate until ready to serve. Remove from refrigerator at least 15 minutes before serving.

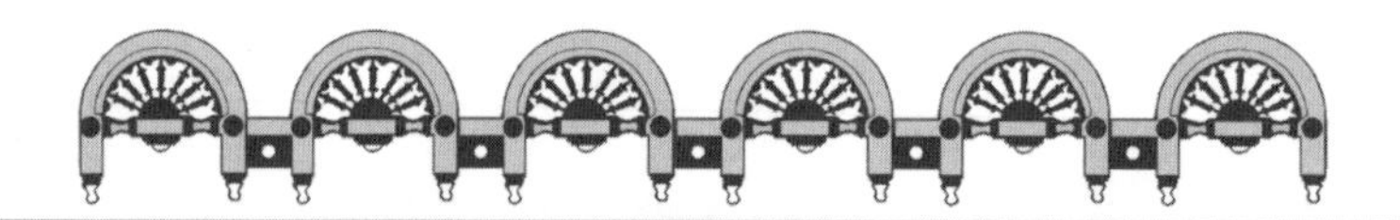

Savory Ham and Cheese Tartlets

Pastry crust
2 cups flour
pinch of salt
1 egg yolk
2 T cold water
½ cup cold butter
1 t lemon juice

Filling
¾ cup grated sharp cheddar cheese
1 cup cooked ham, cubed
½ cup milk
1 egg
oregano and basil (fresh or dried), finely chopped
fresh chopped parsley
salt and pepper to taste

Mix flour and salt; cut in butter with pastry blender until coarse. Stir egg yolk and lemon juice together in small bowl, then pour into flour mixture; add enough cold water to bind together and give consistence needed. Turn out on floured surface and knead several times. Wrap in waxed paper and chill for 30 minutes.

Preheat oven to 350°. Grease a 2-inch muffin pan. Roll out pastry on floured surface. Cut out 12 rounds with a 2½ inch cutter. Line each cup of pan with a pastry round. Sprinkle each with 1 tablespoon cheese. Whisk together egg, milk, salt and pepper. Sprinkle some ham into each cup. Pour egg mixture into pastry shells and sprinkle with herbs. Bake 35-45 minutes or until filling is set. Serve warm.

Yields 12.

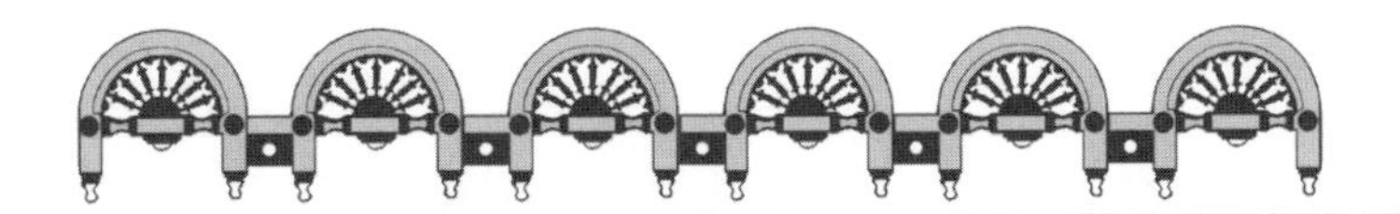

Port Cheddar Spread

- 1 15¼ oz. can crushed pineapple, well drained
- 1 8 oz. package cream cheese, softened
- 2 cups shredded sharp cheddar cheese
- ⅓ cup port wine
- 1 t salt
- ¼ t garlic powder
- ¼ t dry mustard
- 2 T minced parsley

In small mixer bowl, beat softened cream cheese with cheddar cheese and wine at medium speed until blended. Beat in salt, garlic powder and mustard. Fold in parsley and drained pineapple. Pack into lightly oiled 3½ cup mold. Cover and refrigerate for several hours or overnight. Unmold on serving platter and garnish with parsley and serve with assorted crackers.

Yields 3 cups.

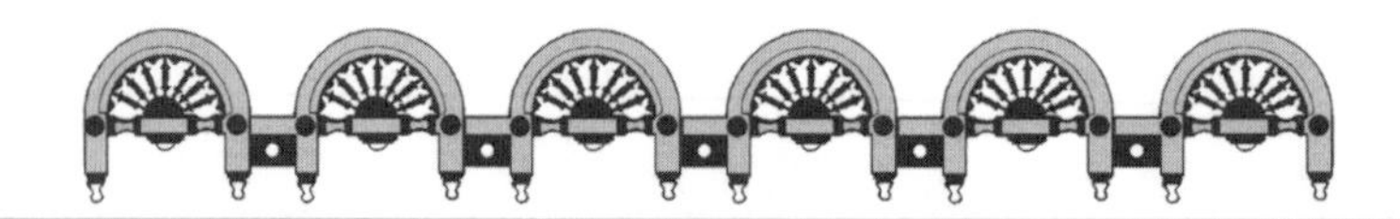

Rum Raisin Cheddar Spread

Delicious with sweet breads or crackers.

Soak raisins in rum for 1 hour. Process cheddar cheese and cream cheese until smooth. Add raisins and rum and blend well.

Yields 1½ cups.

- 1 cup raisins
- ⅓ cup rum
- 1 8 oz. package sharp cheddar cheese, softened
- 1 8 oz. package cream cheese

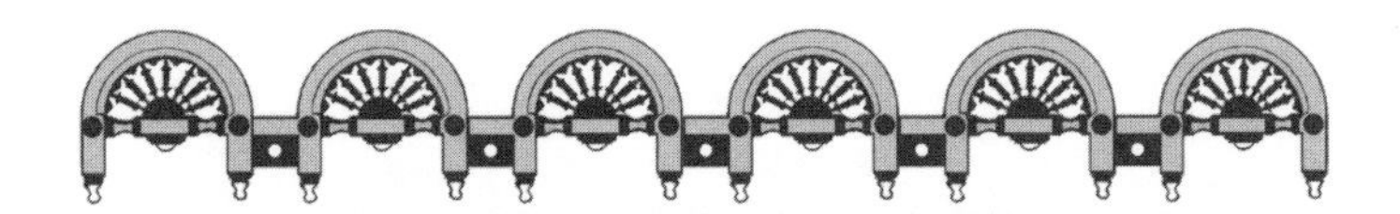

Cheddar & Bacon Log

- 8 oz. cream cheese, softened
- 3 T mayonnaise
- 1/8 t worcestershire sauce
- 1/8 t cayenne pepper
- 2 cups shredded cheddar cheese
- ¼ cup crumbled crisp bacon
- 2 T chopped green onion

Beat cream cheese, mayonnaise, worcestershire sauce and pepper until smooth. By hand, stir in shredded cheese, bacon and onions. Cover and chill for 2 hours. Form into log and roll in toasted chopped pecans.

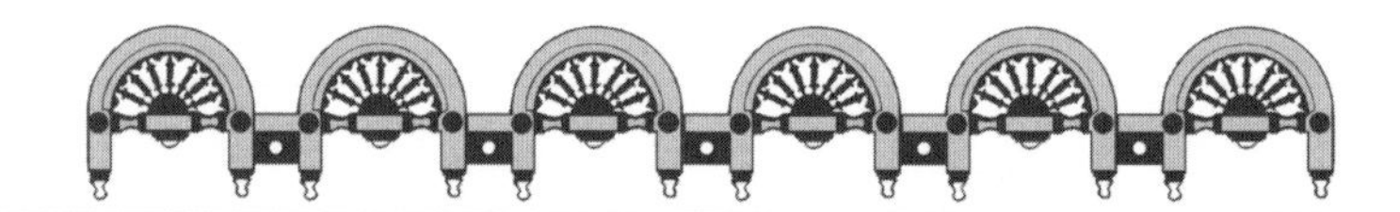

Chicken Salad

Combine chicken breast, celery and grapes and mix well with mayonnaise, sweet pickle relish and lemon juice. Add salt and pepper to taste.

Chill. Spoon onto a bed of lettuce and serve with crackers or sliced baguettes.

- 2 cups cooked, diced chicken breast
- 2 cups chopped celery
- 2 cups seedless red grapes, cut into quarters
- 1 cup mayonnaise
- ½ cup sweet pickle relish
- juice of 1 lemon
- salt and pepper, to taste

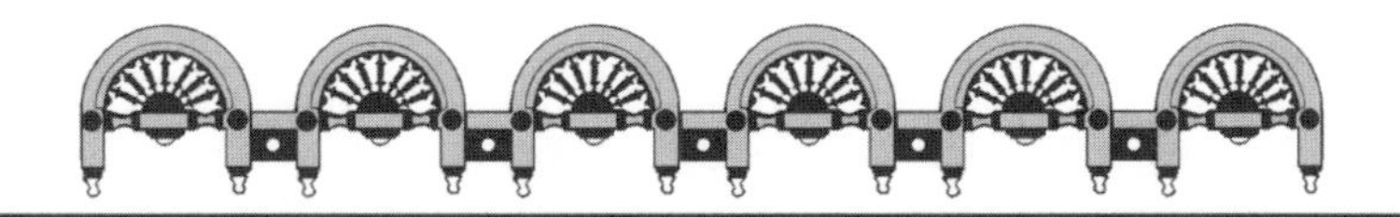

Chicken Salad Puffs

1 cup cooked chicken breast, chopped fine
¼ cup minced celery
¼ cup minced onion
¼ cup chopped almonds
¼ cup mayonnaise
½ t salt
dash of pepper
1 T fresh lemon juice
1 pkg. frozen mini-pastry puffs

Combine all ingredients except pastry puffs. Chill. Meanwhile, prepare the pastry puffs according to directions on the package. Stuff each puff with a tablespoon of chicken salad and garnish with fresh parsley and a grape slice.

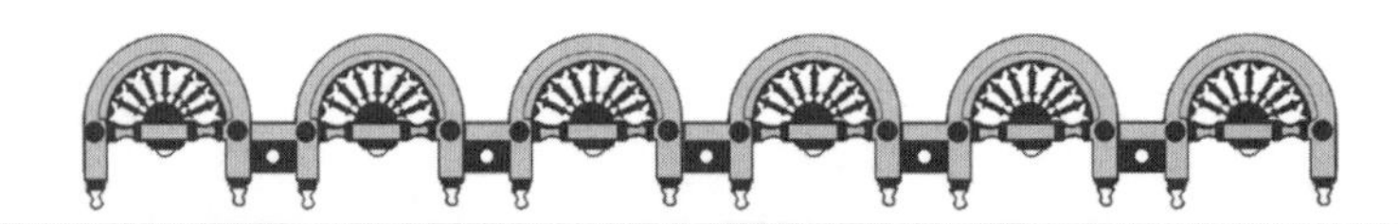

Holiday Brie En Croute

½ package Pepperidge Farm frozen puff pastry sheets (1 sheet)
1 egg
1 T water
½ cup apricot preserves or seedless raspberry jam
⅓ cup dried cranberries, softened
¼ cup toasted sliced almonds
1 brie cheese round (about 1 pound)

This recipe is taken from the Pepperidge Farm puff pastry box. It is easy to prepare and is always a big hit.

Thaw pastry sheet at room temperature for 30 minutes. Preheat oven to 400°. Mix egg and water and set aside. Unfold pastry on lightly-floured surface. Roll into a 14" square. Cut off corners to make a circle. Spread preserves to within 1" of pastry edge. Sprinkle cranberries and almonds over preserves. Top with cheese. Brush edges of circle with egg mixture. Fold two opposite sides over cheese. Fold these two sides onto the round. Press edges to seal. Place seam side down on baking sheet. Brush with egg mixture and bake for 20 minutes or until golden. Let stand 1 hour before serving with crackers or toasted baguettes.

Serves 12.

Note: You can use pastry scraps to cut out fancy designs and place on top of pastry round before brushing the egg mixture on top.

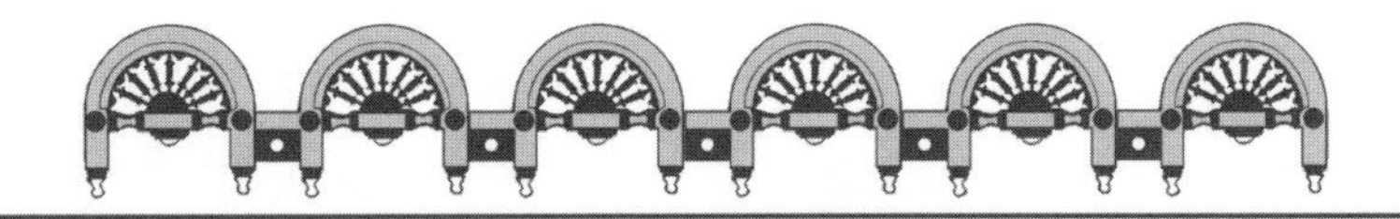

Frosted Grapes

2 t gelatin
½ cup sugar

An attractive garnish for an afternoon tea table.

Combine ingredients in flat bowl. Rinse grape clusters and roll in sugar mixture to lightly coat. Lay on a piece of waxed paper to dry.

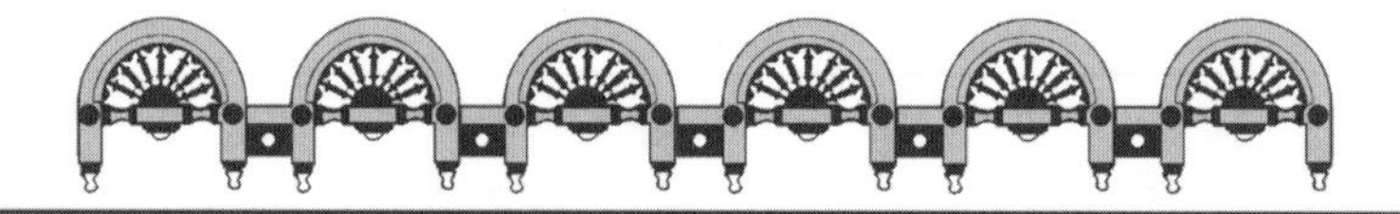

Sweet Dreams: Chocolates on the Pillow & Other Confections

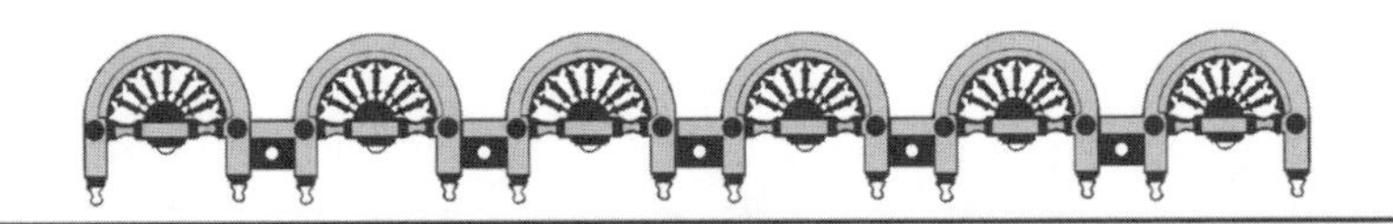

Bedtime Mints

- 2½ lbs. dark chocolate (a good grade bar chocolate)
- 1 lb. margarine (melted and cooled) do not use butter
- 1 t oil of peppermint or any peppermint flavoring

Put melted margarine in bowl of an electric mixer. Melt chocolate to 120° (temperature not to exceed 120°).

Whisk melted chocolate into margarine; mix well. Cool to a soft soap stage (not in refrigerator). Add flavoring and whip with electric mixer until light and fluffy. Pour into 8x12" wax paper-lined pan and refrigerate until set. Make sure waxed paper comes up the sides of pan. When set (several hours or overnight), cut into 1 inch squares and dip into melted chocolate. Mints will cut better if you have a bowl of warm water to dip your knife into.

Serve as a bedtime treat or at teatime.

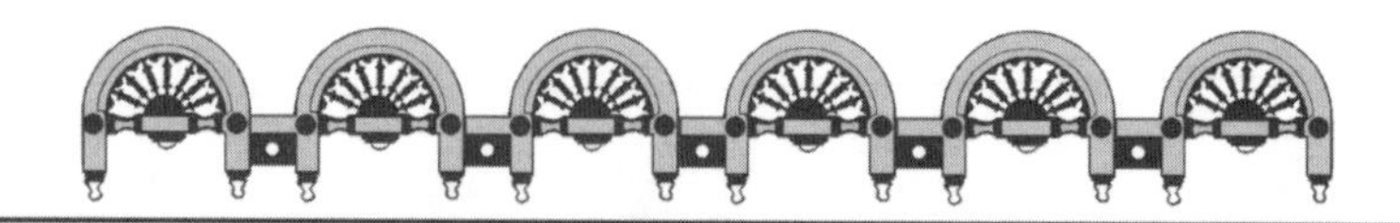

Chocolate-Dipped Rumballs

- 2 cups nuts, chopped (pecans or walnuts)
- 2 T cinnamon
- 2-3 T rum extract or 1/3 cup dark rum
- 2 one pound containers prepared dark chocolate icing
- 1 dark chocolate cake mix

Bake cake mix according to package directions in either a 9x13" pan or a bundt pan. When cake is completely cool, crumble it up into a large mixing bowl. Add chopped nuts, flavoring and cinnamon. Mix well. Add one container of icing and enough of the second container until mixture is moist and holds together after mixing. Cover and chill overnight. Will keep a month in the refrigerator.

Roll into balls and dip into melted chocolate.

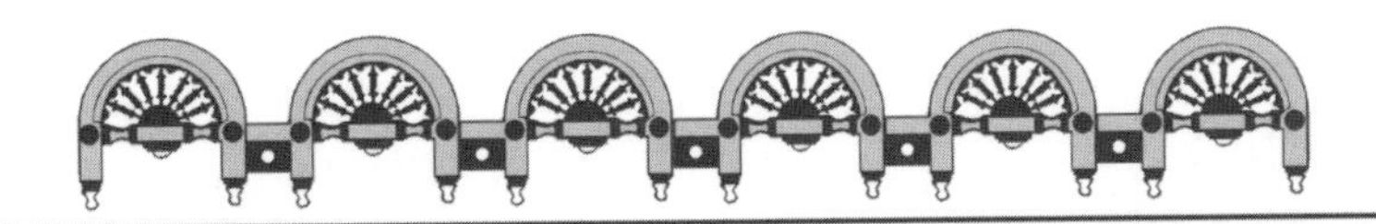

Chocolate Dipped-Maplenut-Creams

- 1 cup heavy cream
- ½ cup milk
- ⅓ cup light corn starch
- 4 cups sugar
- ¼ t salt
- ½ cup Kraft Marshmallow Crème
- 1 T maple extract
- 1 cup coarsely chopped walnuts (optional)
- 1 lb. melted chocolate

In a heavy 4-6 quart saucepan, combine the cream, milk, corn syrup, sugar and salt. Stir over medium heat with a wooden spoon until the sugar dissolves and the mixture begins to boil. Make sure the spoon does not touch the sides of the pan. When the mixture begins to boil, wash down the sides with a pastry brush dipped in hot water to dissolve any remaining sugar granules.

Insert a candy thermometer and cook, stirring occasionally until the mixture reaches soft-ball stage (240°). Remove the pan from the heat, and without stirring or scraping, pour the mixture into a 9x13" baking dish.

Place in a cool area until barely lukewarm. Pour onto a marble slab, and with a wide-blade clean paint scraper, or pastry trowel, work the fondant back and forth for about 10 to 15 minutes. Then add the marshmallow crème, maple flavoring and nuts on top. Continue working the batch until it becomes very stiff and loses its gloss, about 30 minutes maximum. Form into ¾ inch balls. Dip each ball into melted chocolate and set on wax paper-lined tray to harden.

Makes 50 servings.

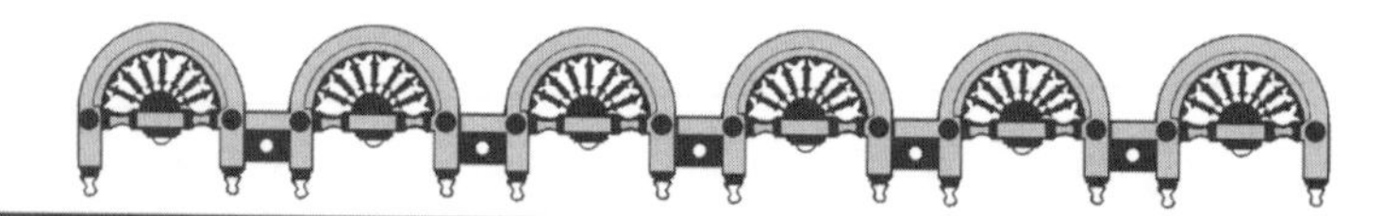

Candied Orange Peel

5 to 6 large oranges
2 cups sugar
1 cup water
Extra sugar for coating
Melting chocolate for dipping

Score oranges with a sharp knife, beginning at top and working down like a spiral at a width of ½ inch. When finished take knife and pull the peel away from the flesh and cut into 4 inch lengths. Repeat with the remaining oranges.

In a heavy saucepan, cover orange peel with cold water the bring to a boil. Remove from heat, drain off the water and repeat the process two more times with filling the pan with cold water and bringing it to a boil When finished you will have boiled the orange peel three times in cold water.

Mix sugar and water and bring to a boil. Add drained orange peel and boil slowly until syrup is almost gone, stirring often. Roll each orange slice in sugar and lay on waxed paper to dry. When dry, one end may be dipped in melted chocolate if desired. When set store in air-tight container.

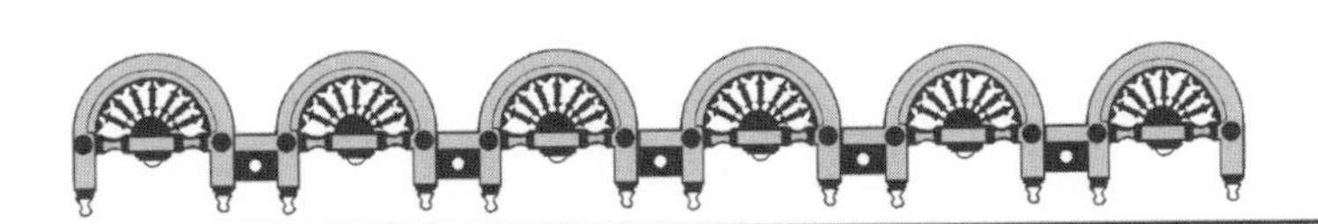

Sherried Walnuts

3 cups brown sugar
1 t cinnamon
1 cup sherry
1 T corn syrup
1/8 t cloves
2-3 lbs. shelled walnuts

Place walnuts in large bowl and set aside. Combine all other ingredients in large heavy pan and cook to softball stage (238° on candy thermometer). Before mixture starts to boil, wipe down sides on pan to get rid of any sugar crystals that have not dissolved. Do Not stir once mixture comes to boil.

When syrup mixture is done, pour over walnuts and toss with wooden spool to coat evenly. Spread out on waxed paper-lined tray and let cool and set. When done, break apart and store in air-tight container.

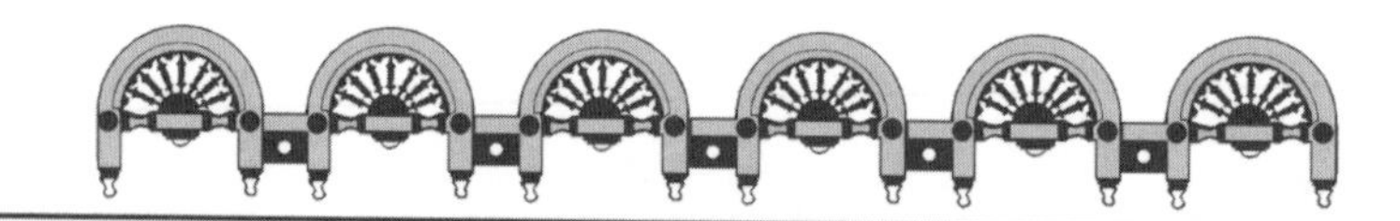

Herbed Spiced Nuts

2 T vegetable oil
1 t dried thyme, crumbled
1 t salt
½ t cayenne pepper
2 cups assorted nuts (almonds, pecans, walnuts)

Whisk together oil, thyme, salt and cayenne. Add nuts and toss to coat well. Spread nuts on baking sheet and roast for 10 minutes in a 350° oven. When cool, store in air-tight container.

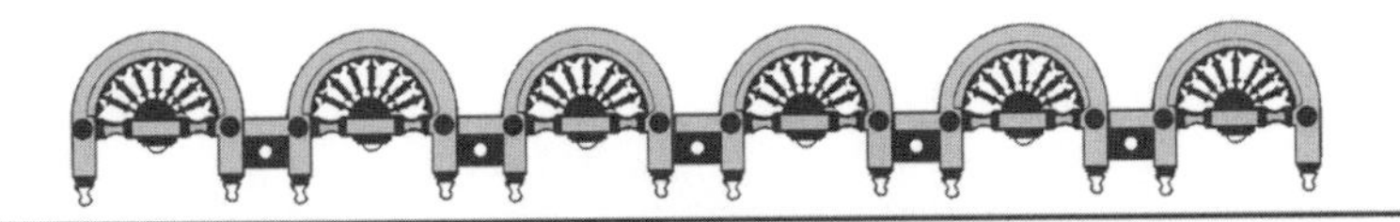

Panforte-Di-Siena

(an Italian Confection)

- 2 cups whole unbleached almonds
- 1 cup candied orange peel, coarsely chopped
- 1 cup candied lemon peel, put through fine blade of a food chopper
- 1 t grated lemon peel
- 1 t cinnamon
- ½ t coriander
- ¼ t cloves
- ¼ t nutmeg
- ½ cup unsifted flour
- ¾ cup sugar
- ¾ cup honey
- 2 T butter
- powdered sugar for coating

Measure the almonds into a bowl and mix with candied orange peel, lemon peel, grated lemon peel, spices and flour. Mix until flour coats each particle. Combine sugar, honey and butter in a deep pan bring quickly to 265° (hard ball stage) on a candy thermometer, stirring frequently. Pour the hot syrup into the almond mixture and blend thoroughly.

Have ready an 8" or 9" cake pan with a removable bottom, buttered heavily, the bottom lined with brown paper, buttered heavily again and dusted with flour. Pour hot batter into pan and spread evenly. Bake in 300° oven for 45-55 minutes until firm in the middle. Cool thoroughly.

Release sides of cake from pan with a knife then invert cake onto large sheet of waxed paper or parchment dusted heavily with powdered sugar. Remove brown paper from bottom, cutting away if necessary. Heavily dust the top of the panforte with more powdered sugar to coat completely and place in airtight container. Panforte can be served immediately or stored airtight indefinitely. Cut into small wedges to serve. Goes well with a glass of Cream Sherry.

Makes about 2½ lb. of confection.

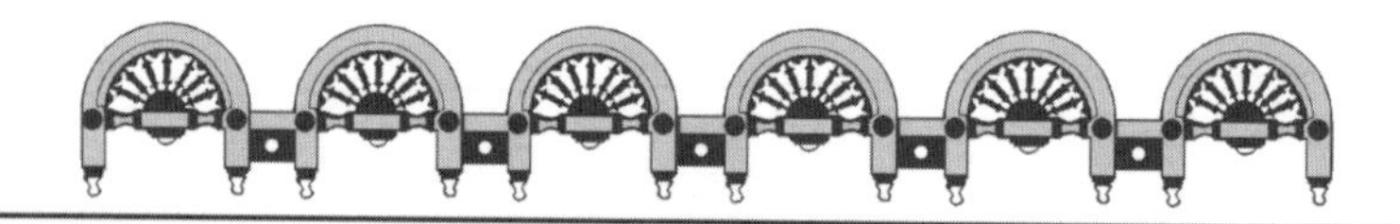

Trade Secrets

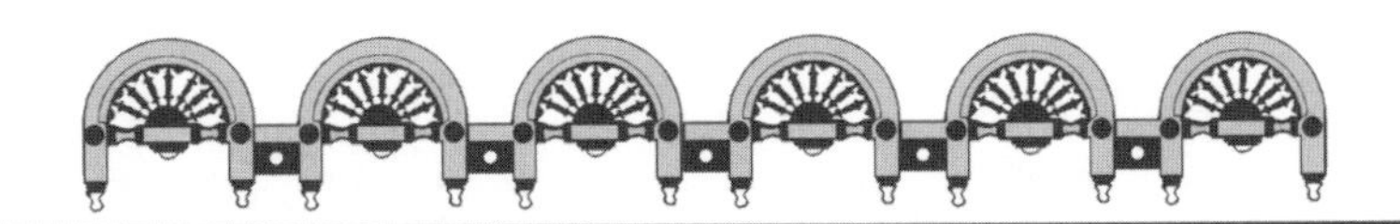

A few helpful hints…

- First and foremost, use only the best ingredients: real butter, fresh eggs & cream and pure extracts and high-quality chocolate. Shop at your local farmers' market whenever possible for the freshest fruit and produce. Using less than the best ingredients will only yield inferior finished product.
- As a rule, I use only unsalted butter when baking. The salt content in butter varies significantly. By using unsalted butter you can accurately control the amount of salt in your recipes.
- Always use large eggs when baking, and if you are making breads or cakes with a high egg content, use brown eggs as their yolks are much richer than white ones. My friend, Julia, who lives just a few blocks from my kitchen door, supplies me with big beautiful brown eggs direct from her chicken house.
- When making pie crust or tart dough, be sure all ingredients are well-chilled, even the flour. This will make your crust extra flaky.
- Use bleached, all-purpose flour unless otherwise noted.
- When making a cake, have all your ingredients at room temperature before starting.
- Always grease your cake, bread or bundt pans with butter rather than a cooking spray. When the recipe calls for dusting the pans with flour, substitute confectioner's sugar instead. If you are making a chocolate cake, dust the pans with cocoa.

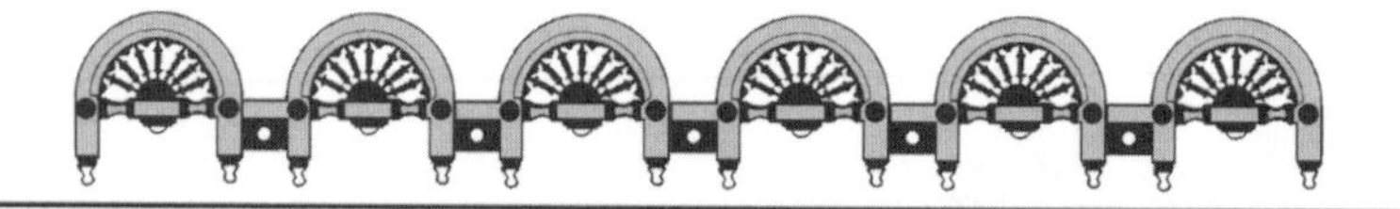